THE FIRST-YEAR
Seminar

Designing, Implementing, and Assessing Courses to Support Student Learning and Success

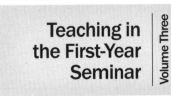

Teaching in the First-Year Seminar | Volume Three

Brad Garner

NATIONAL RESOURCE CENTER

FIRST-YEAR EXPERIENCE® AND STUDENTS IN TRANSITION
UNIVERSITY OF SOUTH CAROLINA

Cite as:

Garner, B. (2012). *The first-year seminar: Designing, implementing, and assessing courses to support student learning and success: Vol. III. Teaching in the first-year seminar.* Columbia, SC: University of South Carolina, National Resource Center for The First-Year Experience and Students in Transition.

Production Staff for the National Resource Center:

Series Editor	Tracy L. Skipper, Assistant Director for Publications
Design and Production	Elizabeth Howell, Graphic Artist

Library of Congress Cataloging-in-Publication Data
Keup, Jennifer R.
  The first-year seminar : designing, implementing, and assessing courses to support student learning & success / Jennifer R. Keup and Joni Webb Petschauer.
    p. cm.
  Includes bibliographical references.
  ISBN 978-1-889271-77-4
  1. College freshmen--United States. 2. College student orientation--United States. 3. Interdisciplinary approach in education--United States. I. Petschauer, Joni Webb. II. Title.
  LB2343.32.K48 2011
  378.1'98--dc22

                    2011015354

Contents

List of Figures

Notes on the Series

I am pleased to introduce the third volume of the series on the first-year seminar to readers. Brad Garner's coverage of teaching strategies is a useful companion to Groccia and Hunter's work in volume II, instructor training and development. Here, Garner delves deeper into the strategies and concepts Groccia and Hunter introduced as they offered advice for preparing instructors to teach in the first-year seminar. In particular, he uses the literature on effective teaching as a springboard for discussions on organizing a syllabus, structuring individual class sessions, engaging students in the classroom, and conducting meaningful assessments of their learning.

The strategies Garner describes are not content-specific, making them well-suited for the more process-oriented approach typical of many first-year seminars. Further, because the strategies are generic, they have wide applicability across the range of first-year seminar courses offered on American college campuses and, indeed, across the entire undergraduate curriculum. While the volume would be an ideal text for use in first-year seminar instructor training and development programs, it is also a useful resource for anyone teaching college students today. I know it will have a place in my teaching library for many years to come.

When I read the first draft of this manuscript in the spring of 2011, I was in the middle of teaching an upper-level English course. I immediately regretted not having read it a month before I started teaching. Holding Garner's ideas about effective teaching and classroom management up to my own course, I recognized the myriad things I could have done differently, could have done better. This is not to say that I thought my course was going badly. In general, the students were thoughtful and engaged. They seemed to like the class. At the same time, I sensed there were things I could do to take my teaching and their learning to a new level.

As I prepared to teach the course a second time in fall 2011, I made a number of adjustments—some of them driven by own assessment of what had not worked as well as I might have liked and some by the strategies described here. For example, I kept Garner's bookshelf strategy in mind as I planned individual class sessions, interspersing periods of lecture or discussion with group activities and reflective writing. In looking at the evaluations for the class, the days where I was able to do this most effectively were successful. In fact, students wanted more activities to balance out discussions of our readings and the very rare lecture I might deliver.

Yet, there is still room to incorporate more of these strategies in my classroom. I have always prided myself on learning my students' names very quickly, but I do not spend much time helping them get to know one another. While I would have incorporated ice breakers and other get-to-know-you activities without a second thought when teaching the first-year seminar, I do not do much beyond first-day introductions in my English classes. However, a student comment late in the semester pointed out the value of engaging in these activities in all courses, especially those in which you hope to have students actively engaged. I cannot remember now what prompted it, but one afternoon Arianne noted that the students in the class did not know each other's names. We took a few minutes to go around the room, introducing ourselves, and then returned to the discussion at hand. When I reviewed the comments on the course evaluation where students wished for more participation in class discussions, I was reminded of Arianne's comment. I wondered whether students would have been more willing to contribute to those discussions if they had *known* their fellow classmates.

In addition to focusing more on community building in my classroom in the future, I will also be revisiting Garner's suggestions on collaborative learning. This is a particularly interesting topic for me, as the course I teach concerns teaching writing at the middle and high school levels. Collaborative learning is a subject we read about and discuss in relation to the students' own teaching practice in the future. The students are typically scoffers, almost all of them recounting a negative experience with group work in the past. Paradoxically, students in the section I taught most recently wanted more group activities in the class, despite their vocal resistance to it. For this course, in particular, I need to invest in strategies that clearly demonstrate the value of group work to my students while offering models they can take to their own classrooms one day. Yet, as Garner notes, the ability to work collaboratively is an important life skill—one that faculty in a variety of disciplines can help students master.

Having recently reread this manuscript and reflected on the application of some of these strategies to my own teaching, it occurs to me that Garner's book is one that requires readers to get their hands dirty. It is not a volume to be read and then placed on the bookshelf. Teaching like learning is an iterative process. It demands that we examine our current practices, incorporate new strategies, and assess the outcomes of those approaches. This volume is an excellent starting point, but it will only take readers as far as they are willing to travel.

I invite readers to get their hands dirty as they use this book to improve their teaching, whether it be in the first-year seminar or another undergraduate course. As always, we welcome feedback on this work, especially as readers discover nuances and valuable innovations of the ideas presented here.

Tracy L. Skipper
Series Editor
National Resource Center for The First-Year Experience and
Students in Transition
University of South Carolina

Overview

Data continue to emerge in support of the first-years seminar as a key element in promoting integrative social and educational experiences, student success, and retention (Goodman & Pascarella, 2006; Kuh, 2008; Porter & Swing, 2006). In the midst of economic uncertainty, increased pressures from accreditation agencies and government regulations for colleges and universities to produce evidence of their effectiveness, and changing demographics within the student body, the first-year seminar will undoubtedly take on added levels of curricular and programmatic significance.

Teaching in the first-year seminar is, in many ways, a great opportunity and privilege (Anderson, 2006). Within the context of the seminar, faculty serve a critical role as they welcome students to campus, build relationships, engage in conversations about the journey that lies ahead, provide guidance on campus supports and resources, and acquaint students with the academic expectations of higher education. The seminar experience can provide ongoing benefits as students progress through their chosen academic programs and move toward completing their degrees.

Teaching in the first-year seminar is also a great responsibility—one that requires instructors to increase their skills in the craft of teaching so they can make a significant difference in the lives of their students. This book is designed to help faculty teach the first-year seminar more effectively by gaining a better understanding of student demographics; plan for the semester-long journey that lies ahead; use a variety of pedagogical techniques designed to promote interaction and engagement around course topics; and construct assessment strategies that are authentic, transparent, and informative. As such, the book opens with a chapter exploring the characteristics of today's learners and the implications for teaching and learning. In particular, chapter 1 explores how generational status (e.g., baby boomer, Gen X'er, millennial) impacts the learning environment, especially when teacher and student come from different generational contexts. The chapter also explores the increased racial and ethnic diversity on college campuses and the growing presence of adult learners.

Chapter 2 highlights three concepts—principles for good practice in undergraduate teaching, the learning paradigm, and pedagogies of engagement—that have transformed our understanding of effective teaching. These concepts are the heart of this book, with later chapters expanding on these ideas.

Good teaching does not just happen; it requires carefully planning, which is the focus of chapter 3. This chapter suggests strategies for articulating learning outcomes, selecting course content, developing the syllabus, and planning a sequence of learning experiences. Similarly, for students to succeed in the first-year seminar—or any course—the instructor must create an environment that supports learning. To that end, chapter 4 addresses issues related to building community in the classroom and establishing standards for civility. However, the chapter also addresses more basic concerns like encouraging attendance, getting students to read assigned texts, and facilitating out-of-class learning.

Drawing heavily on the concepts introduced in chapter 2, the fifth chapter in the book defines alternative approaches to learning and offers specific strategies for actively engaging students in the classroom. Designing, managing, and evaluating group learning experiences (including problem-based learning) and incorporating service-learning in the seminar are major focal points of the chapter.

Technology is a constant presence in our lives and in the lives of our students. Chapter 6 describes a range of technologies and the potential pedagogical benefits and challenges to introducing them in the first-year seminar.

The final chapter addresses strategies for assessing student learning in the seminar. In particular, the chapter encourages faculty to move away from traditional assessments (i.e., objective tests) to more authentic assessments of student learning through presentations, performances, real-world problem solving, portfolios, and so on.

Ultimately, the text is designed as a resource for the creation of engaging and challenging classroom experiences for new college students. While it has been written specifically with the first-year seminar in mind, the principles and strategies described here are easily portable to courses throughout the undergraduate curriculum.

Chapter 1
Understanding Our Students: Current and Future Perspectives

The quality of a university is measured more by the kind of student it turns out than the kind it takes in.– Robert J. Kibbee

These are exciting and challenging times to be teaching in higher education. Exciting in relation to the emerging forms of pedagogy and technology that are expanding the boundaries of teaching and learning. Challenging in relation to the complex collection of competencies our students must gain in order to be effective in the midst of a rapidly changing global ethos. The National Center for Public Policy and Higher Education (2008) conceptualized this challenge and the critical role the academy can play in interacting with the world at large:

> At the outset of the 21st century, a confluence of social, economic, and political forces pose daunting new challenges to the nation's continued vitality . . . . There is little question that higher education must be among the most important intellectual and creative resources assembled to address an array of critical challenges confronting society—including the sustainability of natural resources; the provision of health care for all in a growing, aging population; and the renewal of economic vitality across a wide demographic range, which entails helping more working adults acquire higher-level skills and knowledge, instilling core human values, and strengthening social structures to ensure that future generations experience lives of justice, equity, and fulfillment. (p. 1)

At the center of this confluence we find faculty, students, and the learning outcomes that contribute to a definition of the higher education experience.

What makes this location so intriguing is the fact that as the world changes around us (i.e., the world outside the academy), there are also expectations for change to happen quickly within the academy as the demographics of the student body become more diverse. This new level of student heterogeneity is reflected in a study by Chronicle Research Services (2009) that endeavored to predict the nature of college in the year 2020. Several key predictions outlined in this study provide a wakeup call to colleges and universities as well as a snapshot of the students who will be our partners in learning:

» Although the population of the United States is expected to increase by 10% between 2010 and 2020, there will be a flattened growth trend for the number of high school graduates (with some noted variations across geographic regions of the United States).
» There will be an ongoing decline in the number of White, non-Hispanic high school graduates (11.30%) and Black, non-Hispanic high school graduates (10.07%) between 2010 and 2020.
» There will be a corresponding increase in the number of Hispanic high school graduates (32.98%) and Asian/Pacific Islander high school graduates (58.80%) between 2010 and 2020.
» The fastest-growing market for higher education will be adult learners. This phenomenon will be evidenced by the gradual aging of the population of college students (i.e., from 2007 to 2016, the percentage of 18-24 year-old college students will increase by 11.1% while the percentage of 25-34 year-old college students will increase by 26.8%).
» By 2025, there will be 200 million people worldwide seeking post-secondary learning experiences.

These data have potentially dramatic and significant implications for higher education in general and for faculty teaching in the first-year seminar in particular. Competition for prospective students will necessarily require colleges and universities find new ways to enhance recruitment and services for traditionally underrepresented groups (i.e., Hispanic, Black non-Hispanic, and Asian/Pacific Islander high school graduates), and adult learners. Colleges and universities will also need to consider expanding their recruitment efforts in countries with a history as traditional feeder sources for international students (i.e., India, China, South Korea, Japan, Canada, Taiwan, and Mexico; Chronicle Research Services, 2009). Additionally, these new directions must be pursued in a manner that does not diminish recruitment and services for student groups that have historically served as the primary focus of recruitment and enrollment (e.g., White, non-Hispanic students). This balancing act will be, at best, tricky and challenging.

For the purposes of our discussions in this chapter, we will focus our attention on three elements of this demographic conversation: (a) the generational context; (b) the long-term impact of increased racial, ethnic, and cultural diversity; and (c) the unprecedented increase in the number of adult learners. Within each of these domains, we will review unique learner characteristics, projected trends, and implications for teaching and learning.

Generation as Context

The practice of grouping large numbers of students for the purposes of analysis and categorization can be attributed to Howe and Strauss (1992) who initially defined the characteristics of American generations during the 20th century (e.g., G. I. Generation, Silent Generation, Baby Boomer Generation, Generation X). Playing on this theme, in the book *When Hope and Fear Collide: A Portrait of Today's College Student*, Levine and Cureton (1998) analyzed the life and times of college students of the 1990s. In this analysis of a specific generational group, the authors proposed generations of students, beyond being born at a common point in time, also "live through common momentous events, including wars, political reigns, technological advances, disasters, and economic shifts" (p. 2). These experiences tend to bind together members of a generational group. Coomes and DeBard (2004) illustrate this principle in the following analysis of first-year students in 2003:

> They would have little direct memory of the fall of communism, the first Gulf War, or the Los Angeles riots of 1992. The dominant historical events shaping their worldview were the O.J. Simpson trial, the bombing of the Murrah Federal Building in Oklahoma City, Princess Diana's death, the Columbine High School shootings, and the terrorist attacks of September 11, 2001.... During their lifetime, they only knew four presidents—Ronald Reagan, George H. W. Bush, Bill Clinton, and George W. Bush—but probably only had functional memories of the latter two....
>
> Like the members of their predecessor generation, they too grew up on "Sesame Street," but they also toured the world with Carmen Sandiego. They attended grade school with the Olsen Twins and entered adolescence

with Harry Potter.... They grew up on boy bands like NSNYC and the Backstreet Boys; the grrrl-powered music of Britney Spears, Alanis Morissette, and the Spice Girls; and the rap of Eminem, Lauryn Hill, and 50 Cent.... They moved from CDs to MP3s and are the first generation to hook up through cell phones and instant messaging (IM). (p. 18)

These experiences—both traumatic and mundane—ensure that members of a generation have a common cultural vocabulary, so to speak. For example, two people from the same generation who have never met, come from entirely different parts of the country, and have completely different educational and vocational backgrounds are frequently able to find common ground as they talk about movies, music, favorite actors, fashion trends, popular songs from high school, politics, and memorable moments from history. These connections, or common ground, may be more difficult to establish in cross-generational encounters.

The relationship between differing generational contexts is analogous to two different ways of thinking about the experiences of teaching and learning. First, Giroux (1992) suggests that teaching is analogous to crossing borders from one culture to another. This principle can be illustrated by reflecting on the process of crossing actual physical borders into another country or culture. As individuals make this transition, they immediately become aware of customs, language, and interpersonal subtleties that are different from their own experiences. In an effort to improve their proficiency in this new and unfamiliar environment, they make every effort to acquire those skills that will help them better understand this new setting (e.g., the prevailing language, social amenities, cultural customs) by watching and interacting with those who are citizens of the culture. While learning new skills and perspectives, these border crossers simultaneously make comparisons and connections between what they are learning and observing and their prior experiences. MacBeath (2006), describing his own journey with a group of students, summarizes his experience in crossing borders:

> This simultaneous experience helps us to make a connection. By being able to listen critically to the voices of their students, teachers become border crossers through their ability to not only make difficult narratives available to themselves and other students but also by legitimating difference as a basic condition for understanding the limits of one's own voice. (p. 170)

It is always interesting to sit down with students and share the stories of our lives. These conversations yield new insights and an appreciation for students' journeys, the manner in which they are approaching the college experience, and their aspirations for the future. As we teach, our students will ordinarily come from generations, backgrounds, and collections of experiences different than our own. Giroux (1992) would say an integral part of the teaching process is to cross over into the lives and perspectives of our students in an attempt to see the world from their vantage point. During this interchange, however, it is also important to remember we always maintain a conscious connection to our own collection of life experiences that define who we are as a person.

A second perspective that evokes cross-generational encounters and has implications for working with students in the first-year seminar compares teaching to building a bridge (Kegan, 1994). Bridges are structures firmly anchored on both ends and designed in a manner allowing us to cross over an obstacle as we travel along on our journey. In the same way, Grossman (2009) suggests students should be both encouraged and challenged to move into unknown and challenging terrain as they grow and develop as human beings. Students and teachers collaboratively build a bridge to new insights and understandings. So, although faculty may be in a different generation from their students, they can make conscious efforts to build bridges and promote the connections to learning, growth, and understanding.

During the six-month period when students transition from high school to college, they will likely undergo some of the most significant life changes they will ever experience. For many of these students, this will mean leaving behind high school, moving away from home, enrolling in college classes, and moving into a residence hall (along with a variety of new social and academic experiences). For faculty who are charged with the task of working with students in a first-year seminar, part of the challenge will be to create bridges in the form of dialogues and learning experiences. These bridges will provide a place for students to look at issues and concerns—personal and global—from a perspective different from the one dictated by their own life experiences. In addition, it is worth noting this process can also impact faculty members. By helping students build a bridge between college life and their dreams for the future, faculty members also grow and develop in their roles as facilitators of learning. The hope must be that our students will walk away from course-related learning experiences as different, enriched, and transformed individuals.

This requires that faculty remain open to and embrace that outcome as part of the experience of working with first-year students.

Millennials

Because many of the first-year students faculty encounter will be of the Millennial generation (i.e., those born after 1982), it may be useful to briefly describe their characteristics. Millennials are probably the most analyzed and talked about cohort of students in the history of higher education. With increasing frequency, they have been the subject of books, articles, conversations, workshops, and webinars that have explored their characteristics, quirks, and preferences. This flurry of activity was initially sparked by Howe and Strauss (2000, 2003, 2006), whose work has extensively analyzed, described, and documented the social and behavioral patterns of millennials. In their exhaustive review of the Millennial generation, Howe and Strauss (2000) proposed a range of descriptors to capture their essence and personality:

» Special (i.e., as a focal point of societal and parental focus)
» Sheltered (i.e., under the auspices of helicopter parents)
» Confident (i.e., We can make a difference.)
» Team-oriented (i.e., the good of the group is critically important)
» Conventional (i.e., attracted to traditions)
» Pressured (i.e., working hard to succeed)
» Achieving (i.e., expected and expecting to do great things)

These, of course, are generalizations about a large group of individuals. The list does provide, however, some insight into the nature of this group of students as they enter college.

Interestingly, as a counterpoint to the optimistic view of millennials taken by Howe and Straus (2000, 2003, 2006), Bauerlein (2008) has proposed that the Net Generation (i.e., anyone currently under the age of 30) is, in fact, the "dumbest generation" (p. iii). This position is grounded in the theory that members of the Net Generation have been adversely impacted by the digital worlds of the Internet and social media (e.g., chatting, posting, Tweeting, instant messaging). These readily available sources of amusement, claims Bauerlein, have prompted this generation to avoid ongoing and deeper interactions with art, literature, music, and history. As a footnote, Cooper (2009) reports Bauerlein requires students in his classes at Emory University resort to retro learning by turning off their laptops in class and taking notes by hand. Time will tell whether Howe and Strauss or Bauerlein are correct about the potential and intellectual prowess of millennials. The challenge for faculty becomes one of understanding their learning preferences and adopting a range of teaching techniques responsive to their needs and styles.

Diversity

On any given day, from locations around the world and in our own neighborhoods, we can read and watch reports of disputes and controversies grounded in race, ethnicity, age, socioeconomic status, gender, religion, culture, or sexual orientation. These reports often are discouraging and disheartening. At the same time, however, we can be encouraged as we observe various groups interacting and working together for the purpose of mutual understanding. It is suggested higher education can play a critical leadership role in promoting dialogue and understanding by providing students from varied backgrounds with the opportunity to attend college and develop those skills and dispositions promoting equality, reconciliation, and an appreciation of diversity. This process begins with the first-year seminar.

The term *diversity*, when applied to the college campus, has taken on a variety of new meanings. Historically, this term has been used to describe the percentage of the student body representing various racial, ethnic, cultural, or socioeconomic backgrounds. Shang and Barkis (2009), however, observed this term must now be expanded to include international students; students with disabilities; and gay, lesbian, bisexual, or transgender students. The boundaries of diversity will continue to require refinement and definition as we move through the 21st century (Gaither, 2005).

In light of the projected increases in the overall levels of diversity found on college campuses (Chronicle Research Services, 2009), intentional programmatic responses will be required. Gurin, Dey, Gurin, and Hurtado (2003) suggest there are three separate components to any discussion of diversity on the college campus:

» *Structural diversity*—associated with the numerical representation of various groups of students on the college campus (e.g., racial, ethnic, cultural, sexual orientation)
» *Informal interactional diversity*—related to the relationships students develop with one another with particular focus on interactions between diverse groups of students

» *Classroom diversity*—involving the level at which faculty embrace diversity as a critical concern and integrate knowledge and experiences related to this topic within the classroom

At the level of structural diversity, Hussey and Smith (2010) suggest changing demographics will require colleges and universities expand and vary their recruitment strategies. Yet, the pursuit of campus diversity should always be more than simply a means to meet enrollment quotas in the midst of changing enrollment patterns. Chun and Evans (2009) take this charge a step further by identifying diversity in higher education as an area of critical importance. To realize this goal, and to meet this compelling need, universities will necessarily create wider patterns of service and support for students from varied backgrounds (e.g., ethnic, social, racial, economic, academic).

Structural diversity is only the beginning of the story because colleges and universities must also address the realities of informal interactional diversity. At this level, it will be necessary to confront the reality that diverse groups of students who are entering their first year of college are often brought together rather abruptly and may themselves need to develop new skills and perspectives:

> Attending a college or university may be the first experience of a notably diverse community many students have had. Participation in a community drawn from multiple cultures and experiences calls on an inclination to engage and learn across differences that many students have had no opportunity to achieve. It requires skills that have not been practiced—or valued. (AAC&U, 1995, p. xv)

As a means of creating a viable structure that encourages and supports diversity on campus, there is strong evidence for embracing and developing campuswide initiatives (Chesler, Lewis, & Crowfoot, 2005; Chun & Evans, 2009; Jones, 2005; McLeod & Young, 2005; Raab & Adam, 2005). This requires a systematic plan to develop supports and resources for students and faculty focused on the issues and concerns of diversity. Keup (2008) strongly suggests first-year experience programs must be intentional in the design of learning experiences for participating students as they provide an introduction to the culture of the college campus:

> First-year-experience educators need to identify how their programs, policies, and pedagogies capitalize on the multiple perspectives traditional college students bring to them—perspectives that contribute to the total campus

environment. To facilitate a successful transition for all students, educators should acknowledge elements of the historical and campus context related to the diversity and should understand the impact of institutional messages being conveyed about the value of diversity as it relates to new students' personal identity and interpersonal interactions. (p. 29)

In terms of classroom diversity, faculty members may wonder how to effectively connect course content with discussions, assignments, and assigned readings that address issues of diversity. Such efforts may be complicated by the amount of (or lack of) diversity in a given context. For example, Kazanjian (2000) reflects on the kinds of statements classroom faculty are likely to hear when asking students at her institution to make brief comments about their own cultural and belief traditions:

Colby: I am Baha'i.
Antonia: I am Buddhist.
Desiree: I am a Christian.
Anindata: I am Hindu.
Lisa: I am Jain.
Jackie: I am Jewish.
Yasmeen: I am Muslim.
Simi: I am Sikh.
Allaire: I am Unitarian Universalist.
Sarah: I am Wiccan.
Colby: I believe in the progressive revelation of all prophets.
Antonia: I follow the path of Buddha.
Desiree: Jesus Christ is my savior.
Anindata: I worship Durga, Lakshmi, Saraswati, Krishna, Shiva.
Lisa: I follow the teachings of Mahavirswami and the 23 other Thirthankars.
Jackie: I follow the teachings of the Torah.
Yasmeen: I believe there is no God but Allah, and the prophet Mohammed, may peace be upon him, His messenger and prophet.
Simi: I believe in one God. Waheguru and the 10 Gurus are my teachers.
Allaire: I seek my own truth, drawing from the wisdom of all traditions.
Sarah: The Goddess is my mother. (p. 214)

While such diversity, admittedly somewhat of an exaggeration, could be a disaster in terms of community building in the first-year seminar classroom, it may also give the group permission to explore the things they have in common, to speak freely about their own unique spiritual perspectives, and to journey together on a wonderful exploration of culture and belief. It should go without saying, but an integral part of the classroom diversity component is our ability, as faculty members and individuals, to effectively come to grips with our own feelings, attitudes, and beliefs about diversity. In the classroom, we model, consciously and unconsciously, our own perspectives on the topics and issues discussed. Through our relationships and interactions, we tell the world and our students how we feel and deal with people who are different than we are along some number of dimensions. The classroom portion of the diversity puzzle begins with faculty.

Adult Learners

A 2007 United States Department of Labor publication yields two interesting findings about higher education and adult learners: (a) Adult learners over the age of 24 comprise approximately 44% of U.S. postsecondary students, and (b) the practices and policies of higher education tend to favor traditional-aged students (i.e., 18-21 year-old high school graduates enrolling immediately after secondary school). This information becomes particularly critical in light of predictions that the growth of enrolled adult learners will outpace traditional students by a roughly 2-1 ratio between 2010 and 2020 (Chronicle Research Services, 2009). This could have significant implications for the design and delivery of learning experiences in the first-year seminar.

Interestingly, the predicted increase in adult learners on college campuses is primarily addressed from the perspective of recruitment and adaptation and largely ignores the corresponding issues of teaching and learning (i.e., How might we teach these increasing numbers of adult learners?). Before looking at some of the implications presented by increasing numbers of adult learners on college campuses, it may be helpful to define the variety of dimensions along which adult learners differ from traditional college students. According to The National Center for Education Statistics (2004), adult learners meet one or more of the following criteria:

» Delayed enrollment (i.e., not entering postsecondary education in the same calendar year that he or she finished high school)
» Part-time attendance for at least part of the academic year
» Full-time employment (35 hours or more per week) while enrolled
» Financial independence for purposes of determining eligibility for financial aid
» Dependents other than a spouse (usually children, but sometimes others)

» Single parent status (either not married or married but separated and has dependents)
» Lower academic credentials (i.e., completed high school with a GED or other high school completion certificate rather than diploma, or did not finish high school)

Similarly, Keeling (2004) described adult students as those

> who have been learning all their lives. Many have significant life experience before college (such as marriage, divorce, blending families, work, unemployment, paying bills, caring for relatives, coping with loss, and travel abroad)—and their life experiences have taught and changed them. All of them continue to live lives outside of college itself. These trends, familiar in two-year institutions for decades, are now commonplace in four-year colleges and universities as well. (p. 7)

Each of these criteria has the potential to create a significant impact on a student's response to the demands of college. For example, Fleming and Garner (2009) provide a fictional profile of an adult learner:

> Dawn is thirty-eight years old, a high school graduate, recently divorced, and a single parent. She is employed full-time in a job that she would describe as "tolerable." Dawn views her current job merely as a way to pay the bills. Lately she has been thinking about the need to get some additional training if she is to realize her dreams of owning a home and providing a financially secure future for her children. At a deeper level, Dawn also talks openly about wanting a career that affirms her sense of life purpose and that fully exercises her gifts and talents. In response to these feelings, she has started to investigate the various options that might be available to her as an adult learner. Her priorities include an educational program that will acknowledge her unique life experiences, appreciate the urgency of completing a course of study within a reasonable time and at a manageable cost, and accommodate the many aspects of her life that must be balanced and sometimes juggled as she meets the other demands of her life. (p. 1)

In thinking about Dawn and other adult learners in our classrooms, the following questions become relevant:

» To what extent will Dawn's learning needs and orientation to participation in the class be compatible with the learning needs of the traditional students?

» Are there ways that the instructor can capitalize on Dawn's life experiences in discussions and class activities? Are there circumstances that might lead to conflicts between the adult learners and traditional students in the class?

» To what extent might Dawn's out-of-class life and responsibilities (e.g., family, work, child care) impact her ability to participate fully in this class?

» To what extent should the instructor consider those conditions in setting expectations for Dawn's participation?

Knowles (1984), in the classic work, *The Adult Learner: A Neglected Species*, offered guidance on structuring educational experiences for adult students. Faculty should consider the six key characteristics of adults and their approach to learning, as described by Knowles, when designing classroom-learning experiences. These include the following:

» Adults have a deep need to know "why they need to know."
» Adults are task-oriented in their learning.
» Adults bring to the learning situation a wide range of background experiences.
» Adults have a deep psychological need to be self-directed learners.
» Adults learn best when the learning directly applies to their life situation.
» Adults are motivated by internal pressures (e.g., self-esteem, quality of life).

Much like our other areas of discussion, it is critically important for faculty in the first-year seminar to think not only about the content and process of the class but also the needs, expectations, and orientations of the students. The tools and strategies that follow in this text should provide a resource to assist instructors in this process.

Connecting Points

The first-year seminar is gaining importance as a pivotal element in the promotion of college student success (Kuh, 2008). This fact makes it critically important for colleges and universities to devote significant energy to the design and implementation of high-quality first-year seminars. To be effective, first-year seminars must connect with the learning profiles of the students enrolled while also engaging them in meaningful learning experiences that serve as a gateway to the culture, focus, and learning outcomes of the college experience.

As our campuses become increasingly diverse and welcome students who come to the college experience with varied backgrounds, needs, and interests, the first-year seminar may be where those changes are most dramatically visible (i.e., first-year seminars as the place where campuswide demographics are seen in a microcosm). This fact will require faculty who teach in first-year seminars have a well-developed repertoire of teaching techniques and the ability to think on their feet in relation to selecting and applying those strategies based upon the identified needs of their students.

Chapter 2
Basic Principles of Effective Teaching

If you want to build a ship, don't drum up the men to gather wood, divide the work and give orders. Instead, teach them to yearn for the vast and endless sea.—Antoine de St. Exupery

Teaching in a first-year seminar is an exciting adventure that has tremendous possibilities. Instructors spend critically important time with students as they embark on their college careers. The relationships faculty establish and nurture with students, the enthusiasm they exhibit, the conversations that happen inside and outside the classroom, and the encouragement and accountability they embed within the seminar experience can have a deep and dramatic impact in the lives of new college students. While approaches to teaching the course will be guided by seminar goals and institutional context, including the students served, foundational principles of classroom instruction establish a larger view of professional practice. Three statements describing excellence in educational practice will frame our discussion of the basic principles of effective teaching: (a) Chickering and Gamson's (1987) Seven Principles for Good Practice in Undergraduate Education, (b) Barr and Tagg's (1995) Learning Paradigm, and (c) Edgerton's (2001) Pedagogies of Engagement. This chapter will provide an overview of these foundational principles and how they interact with the focus and purposes of the first-year seminar. An awareness of these principles provides a template for faculty to assess their own collection of teaching techniques and determine specific areas of needed change and improvement.

Chickering and Gamson's Seven Principles

Chickering and Gamson's (1987) seven key principles for promoting the active engagement of undergraduate students in the learning process have been disseminated and reviewed throughout higher education and have been well documented and applied in a variety of settings (Chickering & Gamson, 1999; Newlin & Wang, 2002; Pascarella & Terenzini, 2005). Most recently, they were used as a means of assessing teaching practices in asynchronous Internet-enhanced education and other technological venues (Bangert, 2004; Chickering & Ehrman, 1996; Ritter & Lemke, 2000). These principles continue to be used as a benchmark of best practice.

In their original articulation of these standards for effective teaching, Chickering and Gamson (1987) reviewed their purpose and scope, suggesting "together they employ six powerful forces in education: activity, expectations, cooperation, interaction, diversity, and responsibility" (p. 3). The principles include

>> The importance of ongoing contact—in and out of the classroom—between students and faculty members
>> An emphasis on reciprocity and cooperation among learners in the classroom
>> Teaching techniques focused on active learning
>> A commitment to providing students with prompt feedback on their learning
>> A conscious effort to maximizing students' time on task
>> Consistently high expectations for performance that are clearly communicated to students
>> A healthy respect for the varied ways in which people learn

As such, they strongly emphasize the relationship between the teacher and the learner (i.e., faculty-student contact, reciprocity and cooperation among students, high expectations, and prompt feedback) and the active involvement of learners as they engage with course content (i.e., active learning, time on task, and respect for diverse ways of learning). As a counterpoint, Chickering and Gamson have intentionally neglected to emphasize such factors as disciplinary expertise, test scores, and the accumulation of knowledge as principles of good practice. This does not imply these variables are not significant in the process of undergraduate education. Rather, the omission suggests what distinguishes a mediocre faculty member from a legendary one is the ability to build relationships with students and to promote their active engagement in the learning process. It is probably also safe to speculate that, in the final analysis, actual content-based learning (i.e., the acquisition of learning outcomes, knowledge, skills, and dispositions) flows from a unique interactive relationship between the student, course content, and the faculty member.

The Seven Principles are often presented as an articulation of faculty responsibilities in the creation of an effective environment for learning. Eimers, Braxton, and Bayer (2001), however, have asserted efforts to delineate effective teaching practices must additionally be aligned with the ethos of the campus and commonly held faculty beliefs about expected behavior and performance in the classroom. They further suggest these normative standards can be particularly critical when examining the pedagogical goals and priorities of community colleges, liberal arts colleges, and research institutions. So while it is important for individual faculty members to assert the position that they will engage with the Seven Principles in their own teaching, perpetuation of these practices can either be aided or impeded by campus ethos. In relation to the first-year seminar, therefore, it would be beneficial for faculty to meet on a regular basis to discuss how these approaches to teaching can be implemented and observed in the classroom setting. These types of conversations about teaching can lead to enhanced levels of collegiality, personal accountability, mutual support, and new levels of creativity.

Students as Partners in Learning

Chickering and Gamson, through the language of the Seven Principles, focus their attention on faculty members, students, and administrators as partners in the process of ensuring quality in undergraduate education. Caboni, Mundy, and Duesterhaus (2002) suggest several of the principles (i.e., faculty-student contact, cooperation among students, and high expectations) are directly focused on the level at which students are willing to jointly engage in the learning process. This raises a critical question: To what extent do we communicate and assess the learner's level of responsibility (e.g., willingness to participate, levels of accomplishment, quality of work, engagement with the subject) for what is accomplished over the course of a semester? Quite often, it is proposed, faculty view teaching as something they do *to* the students and not *with* the students. Those two perspectives create entirely different scenarios and bear vastly different results. Perhaps a better way to ask the question is, How can we develop learning experiences that invite learners to engage with the subject, be held accountable for their own performances, but also have the freedom and confidence to take content and assignments in a variety of directions based upon their own interests and learning styles?

The Seven Principles, therefore, seemingly reflect an understanding that the student should be considered a full partner in learning with faculty. The reality of this partnership, and the desire to pursue it over the course of the semester, is a message faculty need to consistently communicate. Rosch and Nocerino (2007) use the relationship between the characters Morpheus and Neo in the film *The Matrix* (Silver, Wachowski, & Wachowski, 1999) to illustrate this point. In the movie, Morpheus is placed in the role of a mentor or teacher for Neo. A dedicated and passionate teacher, Morpheus takes the time to build their relationship and to introduce Neo to the relevance and importance of the subjects they will explore. He takes great care to teach Neo the vital principles and techniques that will become important in his life. As a teacher, Morpheus goes to the next level by facilitating authentic learning tasks that require Neo to actively practice those skills. Morpheus is a teacher with high expectations and a commitment to assuring Neo learn the skills and competencies he will require in the future. Neo is a learner who responds well to those high expectations and who also assumes responsibility for his own learning. It is this level of joint responsibility between teacher and learner that should become the goal of faculty in higher education. There is also strong evidence the influence of Morpheus has encouraged Neo to become a lifelong learner.

A joint statement by NASPA—Student Affairs Administrators in Higher Education and ACPA—College Student Educators International (Keeling, 2004) summarized their aspirations for a collaborative learning environment that includes the student, faculty, and student affairs professionals. Their description of the key values in undergraduate education, in many ways, echoes Chickering and Gamson's principles. Additionally, they reflect on the central role of the student in the learning process. Instead of casting instructional content or the faculty member in the central role, they assert

> We no longer believe that learning is the passive corollary of teaching, or that students do, or should, simply absorb material presented in lectures and textbooks. The new concept of *learning* recognizes the essential integration of personal development with learning; it reflects the diverse ways through which students may engage, as whole people with multiple dimensions and unique personal histories, with the tasks and content of learning. (p. 3)

For faculty in first-year seminars, these principles and associated research have several important implications. First, they are applicable to virtually any academic discipline. The principles also communicate a clear priority on the relationship between faculty and students as fellow travelers on the path to learning, understanding, and meaning making. These elements are critically important in the first-year seminar. Finally, the first-year seminar provides an important venue in which to model and promote faculty-student contact, cooperation among students, and high expectations.

Barr and Tagg's Learning Paradigm

In their now classic article, Barr and Tagg (1995) eloquently captured the differences between a college operating under the auspices of an *instruction paradigm* (i.e., where students are passive recipients of knowledge, and the units of measurement are credit hours earned and the number of classes delivered) and one embracing a *learning paradigm* (i.e., where students and their growth and the construction of knowledge is paramount). The differences between these two perspectives is more than rhetoric and can be observed in the context of institutional mission, the prevailing criteria for student success, teaching and learning structures, valued learning theories, measures of productivity, and the nature of faculty-student relationships.

Pascarella and Terenzini (2005), drawing on the work of Kember and Gow (1994), and using slightly different terminologies, characterized the difference between the instruction and learning paradigms as the difference between "knowledge transmission" and "the development of problem-solving skills, critical thinking [and] independent learning" (p. 59). Students engaged in the learning paradigm are further characterized as deep learners "who have an intrinsic interest in the subject and search for personal meaning in learning activities" (p. 59). Reflections on the differences between a focus on instruction (or knowledge transmission) and learning (or learning facilitation) can be quite sobering and force each of us to look critically at the common practices in our own classrooms and on our campuses.

In a subsequent analysis, Barr (2003) identified five essential features of a campus where the learning paradigm is both valued and evident:

1. *Students are supported in pursuing their own goals.* That is, students have opportunities to fully invest in learning, to discover personal motivations for learning, and to experiment with ideas.

2. *Students engage in frequent displays of learning through participation in authentic assessments.* Such assessments involve students in "tasks that are visible and meaningful to others" (Barr, 2003, p. 155), are experiential, and provide feedback to students.

3. *Students are provided with ongoing feedback.* Barr (2003) suggests feedback both encompasses "the learner's perceptions and beliefs about

their own performance" and "expert guidance" from the instructor (p. 185). The opportunity to give and receive feedback initiates a conversation between the teacher and the learner.

4. *Students view learning from a "long time horizon."* In the instruction paradigm, the time horizon for learning is short—the quiz in tomorrow's class or the exam at the end of the term. Students in the learning paradigm are encouraged to make connections between immediate learning experiences and the long-term big picture. Rather than focusing on learning within a single context, students are also asked to make interdisciplinary connections among their learning experiences.

5. *Students are part of stable "communities of practice."* While the instruction paradigm may emphasize the independence of individual learners, the learning paradigm recognizes that learning is the result of reflective practice in the company of others.

Barr is quick to point out these five features are merely intended to be a blueprint that envisions and frames the parameters of a learning paradigm college. He also indicates the practical implementation of these features may look and feel entirely different across campuses and across instructors on the same campus. Faculty seeking to shift to a learning orientation might first ask themselves, Which of these factors are most evident in their teaching, and which ones may need to be strengthened or enhanced?

Individual and Organizational Challenges

Barr (1998) acknowledged some of the challenges individual faculty members may experience as they engage with the principles of the learning paradigm and consider how to implement them in their classrooms. For example, on many campuses, and in many disciplines, there is a continuing defense of the lecture as the primary and most valid means of teaching. While there is a role for lectures in higher education, they promote passivity and place the student in the role of a spectator. In a similar vein, some faculty members will be unable to fully conceptualize or appreciate the differences between an instructional paradigm and a learning paradigm as modes of operation. To them, what they do is teach and what the students need to do is learn. This is the point at which collegial conversations are helpful in building an understanding of these key concepts. Finally, faculty who espouse the principles of a learning paradigm may experience a sense of cognitive dissonance when they realize they are teaching from an instructional paradigm. It is sometimes painful to look at our own teaching and realize we need to change. Even more painful, however, is knowing change is required without knowing what to do differently.

At the level of classroom implementation, Moroni and Tarr (2005) suggest embracing the learning paradigm may require faculty use approaches grounded in *theoretical eclecticism*. This model requires faculty consciously move beyond a tried-and-true bag of tricks (i.e., things that were successful in the class-room) to one where faculty possess a working knowledge of learning theories (e.g., behaviorism, information processing, constructivism, social constructivism) that affords them the ability to systematically select instructional approaches based on the chosen content and the needs of the participating learners. In practice, this will mean faculty members have the ability to intentionally choose a lecture, discussion, simulation, or assessment task based upon learning theory and not simply because of successful past practice.

For faculty to truly pursue the learning paradigm as a desired outcome, working in the company of others will be a necessity. As each academic year begins, faculty members often head off to their own classrooms and close the door. What happens from that point on is not widely known. The only way we know (or think we know) who are the best professors on campus often comes through an informal network of anecdotes and secondhand comments (or glances at www.ratemyprofessors.com). The teaching we do, although public in many respects, is often a lonely, solitary experience not often discussed with our colleagues. Shulman (1993) admonishes faculty to begin the process of making teaching a "community property":

> I now believe that the reason teaching is not more valued in the academy is because the way we treat teaching removes it from the community of scholars. . . . we celebrate those aspects of our lives and work that can be-come, as we say in California, "community property." And if we wish to see greater recognition and reward attached to teaching, we must change the status of teaching from private to community property. (p. 6)

This observation is an encouragement for faculty to collaborate and share those techniques they have found to be effective in the classroom (as well those that do not seem to work well). In this way, faculty are able to become more effective teachers and bring maximum benefit to students. This level of sharing creates an environment in which faculty can learn from one another and from the experiences of their students.

As an example, Fear et al. (2003) chronicle a process during which a group of faculty members began to explore the intricacies of the learning paradigm and hold one another accountable in moving toward that goal. The authors describe in great detail the transformative yet challenging nature of this experience. Further, they repeatedly articulate the way in which a serious pursuit of the learning paradigm forced them to rethink and redefine teaching practices and old perspectives. This process reveals the fact that striving to be the best possible teacher is a worthwhile goal but one that also requires time, commitment, and an active support system.

In addition, first-year seminar faculty members can be agents of change and growth by engaging their colleagues in discussions about the level at which the learning paradigm is alive and well in the seminar classroom and on the campus in general. As part of these conversations, faculty should consider the possibility of watching one another teach followed by honest, caring conversations about what is seen and heard. While the prospects of peer observations may be frightening, it is critically important in transforming instructional practices.

Moving from the individual faculty to the organizational level, Barr (1998) suggests there are a corresponding number of factors that often inhibit institutions from adopting the learning paradigm. First, it is reasonable for each of us to ask to what degree our institutions really value student learning. Questions that might guide such an assessment include

» When colleagues discuss the nature of the student experience, what is the focus of the dialogue?
» Is the importance of the mission statement as it relates to what students gain from being part of the academic learning community for four years a focus of these conversations?
» Can individual staff and faculty members articulate the unique benefits students derive from the range of learning opportunities currently existing on campus, which supplement and support the academic expectations?

Second, many institutions of higher education fail to grasp the differences between the instruction paradigm and the learning paradigm just as many faculty do. While publicly espousing the values of learning, many institutions are actually living the values of instruction, as evidenced by the types of assessment data collected for the purposes of substantiating the effectiveness of the institution and marketing those accomplishments to prospective students and fellow members of the academy. In an instructional paradigm, assessment data is largely generated on the basis of student participation in objective measures (i.e., true/false, multiple-choice). In a learning paradigm, student performance is measured on tasks involving real-world problems, higher order thinking, authentic tasks, and transparent criteria for success (Chun, 2010).

Next, we can observe the level at which the learning outcomes identified by colleges and universities reflect a focus on instruction or learning. Interestingly, the Higher Education Opportunity Act of 2008 requires colleges and universities use learner-centered criteria to assess their levels of effectiveness: "When evaluating success with respect to student achievement in relation to the institution's mission, the institution includes, as appropriate, consideration of course completion, state licensing examinations, and job placement rates" (Public Law 110-315, Sec. 495). These criteria will, in some ways, force colleges and universities to move beyond a recitation of instructional criteria (e.g., number of majors, faculty-student ratios, enrolled students and growth patterns, recent architectural achievements) to a more focused coverage of those variables directly impact student learning.

As a final observation, Barr (1998) suggests the focus on the instruction paradigm is due, in large part, to higher education's tendency to be a "low-risk, low-feedback, process culture" (p. 23). In practice, this simply means higher education has a pool of students coming forward every year to enroll. Because of this built-in market, there is little motivation to engage in sweeping initiatives that will result in significant change, such as moving from instruction to learning as the primary mode of operation. It is proposed the first-year seminar provides a wonderful environment for faculty and students to experiment with the principles of the learning paradigm. The learning strategies included in this text, particularly in chapters 3-7, have been chosen in relation to their connection with the learning paradigm.

Edgerton's Pedagogies of Engagement

The term *pedagogies of engagement* is attributed to a 2001 white paper focusing on the education projects of the Pew Charitable Trusts, where Edgerton emphasizes the critical nature of learning environments that actively engage students. In an interview with Charles Schroeder (2003), Edgerton reflected on the work being done, and the work yet to be done, to engage students in learning:

> I think that ... we've come to appreciate that the various streams of pedagogical reform—collaborative learning, learning communities,

undergraduate research, problem-based learning, service learning—are all versions of a broader interest in engagement; they are all pedagogies that engage students in new ways. But I'm not sure that many faculty have yet linked these pedagogies to issues of what some people call the "extracurriculum" .... We've got a long way to go to create a total environment that engages students in authentic performances. (p. 13)

In sum, Edgerton is challenging faculty in higher education to think beyond the basics of simply transmitting content to a level at which students are engaged in learning that is deep, meaningful, and integrally connected to the world in which they live.

According to Kuh (2009b), the term engagement has been part of the professional literature for more than 70 years and is currently "used to represent constructs such as quality of effort and involvement in productive learning activities" (p. 6). As an outgrowth of this philosophy, the National Survey of Student Engagement (NSSE) has become the benchmark measure for determining the degree to which institutions are embracing and realizing the goal of engaging students in their own learning. Consider, for example, the kinds of data the NSSE generates in relation to student engagement:

» Academic challenge (e.g., hours spent in preparation for class, the length of papers written, nature of tasks that require making judgments, applying theory, synthesis and organization)
» Active and collaborative learning (e.g., asking questions, making presentations, collaborating with other students, tutoring or teaching others, discussions on assigned readings)
» Student-faculty interaction (e.g., discussing grades with instructor, talking about career plans, collaborative work with a faculty member)
» Enriching educational experience (e.g. cocurricular experiences, practica, internships, study abroad)
» Supportive campus environment (e.g., resources to succeed, support for social experiences, quality relationships)

These are the types of resources and experiences that encourage student engagement. They encompass the entire campus; support students in their learning; include resources from faculty, administration, and student affairs; and help the student look beyond themselves to the community and to the world.

At the implementation level, Mestre (2005) has identified several common elements compatible with pedagogies of engagement, which include (a) students becoming active partners with faculty in the construction of knowledge; (b) faculty serving as coaches and facilitators in the learning process and resisting the temptation to dispense knowledge through monologues or lectures; (c) focusing class time on understanding, exploration, and application; and (d) faculty transitioning from authority figures and experts while students become more self-directed as learners. Additionally, Mestre points out this approach to teaching is often viewed as a counterpoint to more traditional forms of instruction, requiring a thoughtful use of lecture along with carefully crafted discussions, simulations, and reflection.

Smith, Sheppard, Johnson, and Johnson (2005) summarize how this plays out in the classroom:

> engaging students in learning is principally the responsibility of the teacher, who becomes less an imparter of knowledge and more a designer and facilitator of learning experiences and opportunities. In other words, the real challenge in college teaching is not covering the material for the students; it's uncovering the material with the students. (p. 2)

Kuh, Kinzie, Schuh, Whitt, and Associates (2005) takes this advice a step further by delineating specific strategies that can be used to engage students during their first year on campus, such as

» Helping all students spend time interacting with others in a variety of venues
» Structuring the student's initial introduction to campus life
» Making student orientation a balance between academic and social activities
» Linking academic and social activities
» Requiring enrollment in a first-year seminar
» Treating advising as a form of teaching
» Providing experiences that feature interactions with diversity

It is possible, in fact, to think about the first-year seminar as an embodiment of the elements Kuh et al. (2005) have conceptualized as engaging educational experiences: The seminar is interactive in nature; connects students with the campus at-large; blends academic and social activities; provides an introduction to campus life and academic pursuits; helps students build relationships with peers and faculty; often serves as a source of academic advising for students; and exposes students to diverse opinions, experiences, and groups of people.

Connecting Points

It is critically important for faculty teaching first-year seminars to have a firm theoretical foundation that can serve as a basis for the design and delivery of instruction. In this chapter, we have reviewed three of the most enduring perspectives on quality teaching in higher education. These basic principles share several features. First, students' active involvement in their own learning is a central focus. More specifically, active learning entails the design of instructional experiences that call students to collaborate with others, reflect on what they are learning, and demonstrate their learning through participation in authentic assessments. Further, there is an understanding that engaging students in higher education is a team effort, requiring the participation of faculty, students, administrators, and student affairs personnel.

The first-year seminar, in its design and implementation, must include provisions for learning environments that fully engage students. As such, instructors are encouraged to review these basic principles of teaching and use them as a rubric for evaluating the design and delivery of learning experiences. Such an evaluation should prompt instructors to ask, To what extent does the learning environment align with the theoretical foundations of teaching in the first-year seminar? Areas of close alignment might suggest strengths, while places where practice diverges from these principles may suggest areas for improvement. This process of self-examination, as an ongoing part of the teaching and learning process, is the first ingredient of achieving excellence.

Chapter 3
Planning for Instruction in the First-Year Seminar

A good plan is like a road map: It shows the final destination and usually the best way to get there.—H. Stanley Jones

A semester spent teaching a first-year seminar is a journey of grand proportions. Although there will always be surprises and unexpected opportunities along the way, it behooves faculty to invest time and energy in planning a comprehendible and cohesive learning experience. Bain (2004), in his analysis of what the most effective college teachers do, made the following observation about the process of preparing to teach:

> the best educators thought of teaching as anything they might do to help and encourage students to learn. Teaching is engaging students, engineering an environment in which they learn. Equally important, they thought of the creation of that successful learning environment as an important and serious intellectual (or artistic) act, perhaps even as a kind of scholarship, that required the attention of the best minds in academia. (p. 49)

To that end, this chapter addresses several critical issues in planning for a successful instructional experience in the first-year seminar, including articulating learning outcomes, determining course content, developing the course syllabus, and planning the sequence of learning experiences.

Learning Outcomes

Like any journey, course planning must always begin with serious consideration of the final destination. Faculty should ask themselves, What types of knowledge, skills, and dispositions do I plan for my students to learn and accomplish over the course of this semester as a direct result of taking this course? By answering this question, faculty can then make informed decisions about the selection of textbooks, assignments, classroom and out-of-class learning experiences, and assessment strategies. Learning outcomes are measurable objectives of the knowledge, skills, and dispositions we plan for students to acquire and accomplish over the course of their first-year seminar (Gahagan, Dingfelder, & Pei, 2010). From this brief description, several key factors become apparent:

» Learning outcomes are about what students will learn and not what the faculty member will do.
» Learning outcomes must be written in a manner inviting measurement of student performance.
» Learning outcomes are the cornerstone of the planning process. Once learning outcomes have been articulated, faculty can then move to a delineation of lectures, discussions, assignments, service-learning experiences, simulations, and readings that will facilitate student learning and the accomplishment of identified outcomes.

First-year seminars take on a variety of forms in colleges and universities, including extended orientation seminars, academic seminars with generally uniform content across sections, academic seminars on various topics, preprofessional or discipline-linked seminars, basic study skills seminars, and hybrids that combine elements of two or more seminar types (Hunter & Linder, 2005). Although first-year seminars come in a variety of flavors, they do tend to have some commonalities in relation to their focus:

First-year seminars facilitate learning: learning about a subject or combination of topics, learning about the institution, learning about diversity within campus communities, but most important, learning about oneself and one's abilities. The very nature of first-year seminars allows faculty to facilitate the growth and development of students while still being flexible enough to accommodate the campus-specific issues that an institution believes are important. (p. 276)

On some campuses, there may be specific learning outcomes universally applied across the campus to all first-year seminars depending upon the chosen model. Porter and Swing (2006) report these learning outcomes are often clustered in the areas of study skills and academic engagement, college policies, campus engagement, peer connections, and health education. On other campuses, there may be a variety of learning outcomes that capture the essence of the first-year seminar experience but also integrate a focus on cultural, disciplinary, or interdisciplinary content. These are largely local decisions that can be facilitated and guided by campus culture and best practices as articulated in the professional literature.

A Framework for Thinking About Learning Outcomes

When thinking about the design of learning outcomes for a first-year seminar, it is helpful to have a framework guiding this selection process. As an example, consider the levels of thought and activity outlined in Bloom's Taxonomy. Benjamin Bloom (1956) led a group of educational psychologists in creating a hierarchy of intellectual behaviors that can occur during the learning process (i.e., from simple to complex levels of thought and activity). The hierarchy was later revised by Anderson and Krathwohl (2001). This most current hierarchy identifies a variety of learning tasks, from simple to complex, and includes

- » Remembering (e.g., simple recall of facts, figures, names, and dates as often measured by true/false and multiple-choice assessments)
- » Understanding (e.g., grasping the meaning of read or heard materials)
- » Applying (e.g., using previously learned materials in new situations)
- » Analyzing (e.g., breaking down materials into component parts)
- » Evaluating (e.g., judging the value or quality of something based upon specific criteria)
- » Creating (e.g., using current knowledge, information, and skills to invent something new and different)

Anderson and Krathwohl (2001) encourage teachers to think seriously about the design of instructional experiences and assessment strategies that move beyond a simple recall of facts and require students to use higher level thinking skills. Unfortunately, many college classes typically focus on the recall of facts and simple levels of understanding. The following critical questions help instructors move beyond this level toward learning experiences emphasizing analysis, evaluation, and creation:

» Where do the learning outcomes, teaching strategies, questions, and assessments fit into the hierarchy of intellectual behaviors?
» How might the course be revised to encourage students to engage in higher order thinking?
» Do classroom learning experiences and assessments stretch students to engage in higher order thinking?

The delineation of course learning outcomes is often viewed as an onerous and difficult task. Most faculty would agree it is critically important but do not feel they have adequate skills or training in the crafting of these outcomes. Diamond (1998) suggests a strategy for completing this process in a painless manner:

> As an alternative to writing objectives [learning outcomes] in the abstract, a facilitator can help us develop strong, clear objectives by playing the role of the student asking us, "If I'm your student, what do I have to do to convince you that I'm where you want me to be at the end of the lesson, unit, or course?" Out of this discussion will come performance objectives that are measurable and that tend to be far more important and at a higher level than would be produced otherwise. (p. 135)

While this may sound like a simple exercise, most faculty probably engage in the process of learning outcome creation by themselves with little feedback from peers in their own or other disciplines. Further, once learning outcomes are created, it is very likely they remain the same semester after semester. Completing this type of exercise in the company of colleagues who are also teaching can help participants clarify their own thinking while also receiving constructive feedback on what makes sense and what needs to be refined and modified.

Determining Course Content

As described above, the articulation of learning outcomes is the first step in course planning. A related task is the process of determining exactly which collections of content will be included in the course. In the midst of a time when new information is being generated at a daunting rate, faculty members are often faced with the dilemma of what to leave in and what to take out of course content. For some academic disciplines and professional preparation programs, this question is answered rather easily and directly in the form of accreditation standards and qualifying examinations. On many campuses, first-year seminars have a common set of learning outcomes, assignments, and experiences to guide such decision making. At the same time, faculty members maintain a level of autonomy in deciding how they actually teach the seminar. Given that level of autonomy, what are the criteria that can or should be used to make these important instructional decisions?

One way to answer this question is to consider the possibilities for course content as a series of three boxes. The largest of the three boxes contains all of the knowledge and information that has been generated in a particular academic discipline. The contents of this box, and its size, continues to grow and expand as new discoveries are made and extend the boundaries of existing knowledge.

As hard as we might try, there is no possible way for any faculty member to acquire all of the available knowledge in his or her academic discipline—or to remain fully abreast of every new theory, discovery, article, book, or conference presentation. Therefore, the second box is a bit smaller than the first. It contains all of the knowledge, skills, and dispositions that individuals have acquired and mastered within their specific disciplines over the course of their careers. This box also grows and expands as they read, attend conferences, and engage in scholarly pursuits. Although constantly growing, this box will never be as large as the first one.

The third box is designed to hold the content of individual courses (i.e., the knowledge, skills, and dispositions students are expected to learn over the course of a semester). This box is smaller than the other two as we cannot possibly teach students, within the context of one course, all of the information we know individually or that may be known collectively within an academic discipline. It is at this point the real challenge arises: picking and choosing instructional content and learning outcomes that will form the foundation for the learning experiences comprising a course. Figure 3.1 offers several possible sources of course content. Faculty who are designing or refining a course syllabus will want to think about which of these sources they consider to be valid, reasonable, and defensible. Moreover, such evaluations should be included in regular discussions on campus and become an integral part of the campus culture.

Consider the courses you are teaching this semester. Which of the following criteria do you consider relevant, or do you employ, when selecting course content?

_____Course syllabi developed by faculty who previously taught this course

_____A systematic review of the professional literature

_____An intuitive feeling the content "just seems to make sense"

_____Organizational structures and course content provided by textbook publishers

_____Materials downloaded from the Internet

_____Content you were taught when you took this or a similar course

_____Insights gained through conversations with valued colleagues

_____Learning outcomes mandated through accreditation agencies

_____The fact that it is what you have always done—and it always seems to work

Figure 3.1. Varied approaches to choosing course content.

Developing the Course Syllabus

Erickson, Peters, and Strommer (2006) provide an interesting perspective on the importance of the first class of the semester and rolling out the course syllabus. As they note, students "want information about the course—the content, the requirements, the evaluation procedures, and so on. These matters constitute the explicit agenda for the first class meeting. A good syllabus helps address these issues" (p. 67). In fact, the ceremonial first pitch of every semester is a review of the course syllabus, as faculty go over and outline the important things to remember and offer advice on how to be successful in the class. Yet, there is a healthy amount of skepticism among faculty as to how much this ceremony actually accomplishes and to what degree students remember any of the helpful hints dispensed for their well-being and edification. A study by Becker and Calhoon (1999) surveyed students in an introductory psychology class to determine which features on course syllabi drew the greatest and least amount of attention. The top five items retained by students included (a) examination or quiz dates, (b) due dates on assignments, (c) reading materials covered by each exam or quiz, (d) grading policies and procedures, and (e) the types of exams and quizzes (e.g., multiple-choice, true/false). The items that were least remembered were (a) available support services, (b) the instructor's office hours, (c) the academic dishonesty policy, (d) course information (i.e., number, title), (e) withdrawal dates, and (f) the titles and authors of textbooks. It would appear from the results of this study, students take a very utilitarian approach to the syllabus with a primary focus on what will have the greatest potential impact on their final grade.

Thus, a question that might emerge from the Becker and Calhoon (1999) study is, What might we do as faculty to make our syllabi more memorable and useful? As routine as this process may sound, or even become, the development of thorough, complete, and well conceived course syllabi can provide the groundwork for a successful semester of learning. According to Littlefield (1999, as cited in Slattery & Carlson, 2005), there are seven major functions of the course syllabus, which include

» *Setting the tone for the course.* A well-developed course syllabus sends the important message that the faculty member has given serious thought to course organization and delivery. A syllabus that is attractive, well organized, and captures the interest of students from the first day of class will pay benefits throughout the entire semester.

» *Motivating students to set high goals for themselves.* If students sense the instructor's excitement, passion, and commitment to the content of the course,, they are more likely to be willing to stretch themselves to achieve and produce. The syllabus is an invitation to students to give their best efforts in exchange for the instructor's best efforts.

» *Serving as a planning tool.* A high-quality syllabus sets forth the teacher's big-picture game plan for the semester. The development of the course syllabus affords faculty members the opportunity to plan instructional strategies for the semester.

» *Providing a structure for student work.* Instructional faculty are competing for the time, interest, and energies of their students. A well-conceived syllabus communicates expectations that students will invest themselves in meeting the learning requirements of the particular course. This provision also encourages students to look ahead and plan effective ways to complete assigned tasks.

» *Helping faculty plan and meet course requirements and expectations.* Planning time spent in advance of the semester (e.g., order of approaching topics, timing of assignments, planning in regard to instructional activities) will pay dividends in the quality of teaching. Once instructors have a sense of where they are headed, they can lead student learning in that clear direction. This takes planning to a more detailed level.

» *Providing a contractual arrangement between faculty and students.* Any disagreements that may arise concerning grading practices, due dates, and attendance policies can be referred back to the stated course policies and procedures. In fact, Wasley (2008) likens the syllabus to a prenuptial agreement. As students become more prone to filing complaints with academic administrators and even to litigation (e.g., I deserve a better grade and my parents are contacting their attorney.), there is a tendency to view the syllabus as a preemptive contract in which faculty articulate every possible scenario as a protection strategy rather than as means of communicating with students.

» *Becoming a portfolio artifact for tenure and promotion.* As time passes and faculty prepare for tenure and promotion review, course syllabi serve as a means to document the quality of teaching and strategies for addressing students' learning needs.

Content and Format of the Course Syllabus

The course syllabus might also be seen as a tool for helping students succeed in the course. Habanek (2005) examined the level at which a sample of syllabi consistently presented information about course outcomes, required materials, the schedule of classes and activities, success criteria for the course, expectations for civility, and the instructor's enthusiasm for the course. Based upon the tremendous level of variability (e.g., multiple omissions), Habanek concluded the syllabi raised serious questions about the integrity of these documents as a means to promote student success. Thus, if the syllabus is to be a useful tool for students, it is reasonable to expect it to contain a number of basic elements in all circumstances. For the purposes of this discussion of the first-year seminar, a sample list of key elements to include in a syllabus has been summarized in Figure 3.2.

___ General Information: This introductory section of the syllabus provides such basic information as the course title, section number(s), classroom location, dates and times of class meetings, and faculty contact information (e.g., telephone numbers, e-mail addresses), required texts and course materials and your office hours.

___ Course Rationale: This is your opportunity to share the reasons why this course is a critically important and how the content connects with the life and learning experiences of your students.

___ Your Passion and Purpose in Teaching This Course: In this section of the syllabus, you have an opportunity to share your personal and professional passion for this course and the things that will be taught and learned. Share your heart and your faith with your students.

___ Course Objectives: Articulate the knowledge, skills, and dispositions that you believe are important for your students to master over the course of this semester.

___ Topical Schedule: How do you plan to approach the breadth and depth of the topics that comprise this area of study? In this section of the syllabus, provide your students a dated schedule of the topics that you will be sharing and learning about on this semester-long adventure.

___ Course Reading: Students are not genetically and naturally inclined to read required course materials. Through your prompting and systematic planning, however, they can be encouraged to see the value of reading along as they are learning.

___ Course Products: Students need to know in detail what it is that you will expect them to produce this semester, the parameters of those assignments, and when they are due to be completed. Although some may choose to procrastinate, for others it gives an important target date for task completion.

___ Assessment Scheme: "Will this be on the test?" is a common refrain of the college classroom. Prepare in advance for the assessment strategies that you will use (e.g., quizzes and examinations, research papers, group projects, presentations, online activities). Provide your students with information on these tasks and their relative levels of importance (e.g., point values).

___ Course/University Policies: What are the policies and procedures that your students need to understand as they enter this course? Examples include attendance procedures, reasonable and acceptable absences, and cheating/academic dishonesty. Spell these out in your syllabus or give reference points so that students can remain well informed.

___ Motivational Thoughts: As an added touch, consider the use of graphics and text boxes with quotes that connect with your course and your teaching.

___ Additional Resources and Assistance: Provide students with resources or information on how to get additional assistance they may need, appropriate Internet links, and campus resources that will assist in their learning.

Figure 3.2. Syllabus preparation checklist. Reprinted from *A Brief Guide for Teaching Millennial Learners* by J. B. Garner, 2007, p. 19. Copyright 2007 by Triangle Publishing. Used with permission.

Another aspect of syllabus development to keep in mind is these documents are always a work in progress. While it may be tempting to simply do a *find and replace* to update dates and times from one semester to the next, instructors are encouraged to examine the syllabus with a fresh eye and to incorporate one or two new enhancements that will promote student learning. For example, instructors might consider formatting the syllabus in a unique way. The promising syllabus, graphic syllabus, and interactive syllabus—described in greater detail below—are just a few examples.

The promising syllabus. Bain (2004) describes a process for creating a syllabus that contains three major components:

» A description of the promises and opportunities that will be available to students over the course of the semester (e.g., new skills and abilities). This first component serves as an invitation to a feast, giving students control over the level at which they choose to partake of this upcoming opportunity.

» An explanation of what students will be doing to realize the aforementioned opportunities. From a more traditional perspective on the syllabus, this would include readings, class activities, and assignments.

» The syllabus also initiates a conversation on how the students and the faculty member can and should interact over the course of the semester. Bain suggests this is about more than outlining grade policies. Rather, it is

> the beginning of a conversation that should last throughout the term that will help students understand what it means to become an "A" thinker in a particular course or discipline, and what constitutes evidence that the student has achieved that kind of thinking. (as cited in Lang, 2006, p. B114)

The graphic syllabus. This unique and creative approach to syllabus development demonstrates to students the connections and interrelationships (i.e., spatial, temporal, and organizational) between the various components of a course (Nilson, 2007). By using icons, pictures, lines, and arrows, students are literally given a picture of what lies ahead over the course of the semester. In essence, a traditional syllabus provides a word-based description of the semester; the graphic syllabus offers a pictorial view of the semester and the relationships between various course components. A sample graphic syllabus for a course on teaching and learning is illustrated in Figure 3.3.

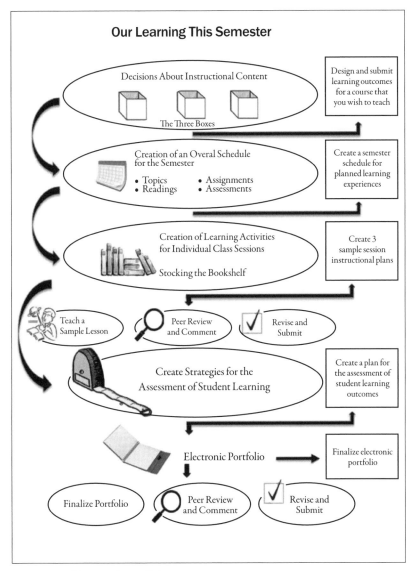

Figure 3.3. The graphic syllabus.

Nilson and Biktimirov (2003) suggest the graphic syllabus has many inherent advantages, including its appeal to students with a nonverbal learning style. The graphic representation exposes students to a different type of learning tool, which may lead to better encoding of the information for long-term memory. The graphic symbols make the relationships between topics and course components explicit, and having to visualize those relationships, forces faculty to think differently about the various elements of the course and the ways in which those various pieces are connected or related. Finally, the development of a graphic syllabus can be a creative endeavor for faculty, enhancing the overall course design process.

The interactive syllabus. In the midst of an increased emphasis on the use of electronic media, the interactive syllabus provides an engaging way to capture the interest of students. A syllabus that includes a variety of links and interestgrabbers, such as publisher websites, information for organizations or affiliations, course or program information, reference materials for weekly discussion, clever graphics, audio clips or podcasts, video clips (e.g., YouTube), Facebook sites, and photographs may generate more student excitement than a traditional, text-based syllabus (Magna Publications, 2005). This type of adjustment makes the syllabus more than simply a course schedule or a way of keeping track of assignments and tests. Rather, it becomes a living document as illustrated in Figure 3.4.

In addition to paying attention to syllabus design, faculty may consider other strategies for generating student interaction and engagement with the course syllabus. Two such strategies follow.

QwikFax. As we move deeper into a digital culture, and as students are required to track greater numbers of electronic resources, an intermediate step in organizing data is the QwikFax strategy. This strategy balances the value of placing materials into electronic venues (i.e., environmental sustainability, greater levels of flexibility in the design of course materials, easily accessible, redundancy of course materials) with the reality of student challenges in organizing information from a variety of sources. The QwikFax is a one-page directory of the resources available in the class (e.g., syllabus, video clips, online reading, online quizzes), where they are located, and how they can be accessed. This document (as the only one actually distributed in hard copy during the first day of class) guides the discussion about the course, its learning outcomes, and learning experiences. As an added bonus, when a student asks a question about the timing of an examination or an article they need to read, he or she can be referred to the QwikFax document (which is also posted on the web) as a means of gaining the necessary information.

Links to Resources for This Semester	
Decisions About Instructional Content	
Learning Outcomes	Garner, J. B. (2007, January). Learning outcomes and expectations, *The Toolbox*, 5(1). Retrieved from http://u101tech.sa.sc.edu/NRC/toolbox/output/archive/files_pdf/05_01.pdf
Instructional Design	Spence, L.D. (2001). The case against teaching. *Change, 33*(6), 10-19.
Creation of an Overall Schedule for the Semester	
Planning the Syllabus	Habanek, D. (2005). An examination of the integrity of the syllabus. *College Teaching, 53*(2), 62.
	Garner, J. B. (2006, January). Building a syllabus. *The Toolbox, 4*(1). Retrieved from http://u101tech.sa.sc.edu/NRC/toolbox/output/archive/files_pdf/04_01.pdf
Mapping the Semester	Nilson, L. B., & Biktimorov, E. B. (2003). Mapping your course: Developing a graphic syllabus for introductory finance. *Journal of Education for Business, 78*(6). 308-312.
Creation of Learning Activities for Individual Class Sessions	
The Learning Paradigm	Barr, R. B., & Tagg, J. (1995). From teaching to learning: A new paradigm for undergraduate education. *Change, 27*(6), 12-25.
The Bookshelf	Smith, K.A., Sheppard, S.D., Johnson, D.W., & Johnson R.T. (2005). Pedagogies of engagement: Classroom-based practices. *Journal of Engineering Education, 94*, 87-101.
Organization of Teaching	Garner, J. B. (2006, February). Organizing teaching to promote learning. *The Toolbox, 4*(2). Retrieved from http://u101tech.sa.sc.edu/NRC/toolbox/output/archive/files_pdf/04_02.pdf
Active Learning	Gier, V., & Kreiner, D. (2009). Incorporating active learning with PowerPoint-based lectures using content-based questions. *Teaching of Psychology, 36* (2), 134-139.
The Physics of Teaching	Garner, J. B. (2008, September). The physics of teaching. *The Toolbox, 6*(4). Retrieved from http://u101tech.sa.sc.edu/NRC/toolbox/output/archive/files_pdf/06_04.pdf
Technology	Weaver, B., & Nilson, L. (2005). Laptops in class: What are they good for? What can you do with them? *New Directions for Teaching & Learning, 101*, p3-13.
Assessment of Student Learning	
Alternative Assessment	Backes, C., & Brown, P. (2009). Going beyond the test! Using alternative assessments in career education. Techniques: *Connecting Education & Careers, 84*(3), 34-37.
Rubrics	Garner, J. B. (2010, October). The rubric: A tool for authentic assessment. *The Toolbox, 9*(2). Retrieved from http://u101tech.sa.sc.edu/NRC/toolbox/output/archive/files_pdf/09_02.pdf
	Andrade, G. H. (2005). Teaching with rubrics: The good, the bad, and the ugly. *College Teaching, 53*(1), 27-30.

Figure 3.4. The interactive syllabus.

The syllabus quiz. As a way of encouraging students to become knowledgeable about the first-year seminar and the expectations and experiences of the semester, it is always helpful to conduct a syllabus quiz at the end of the first week of class. This can be done in the classroom or online and focuses on the basic information about the course students need to have to maximize their probabilities of success during the semester. This practice points students to the importance and breadth of information included in the syllabus.

Flexible due dates. Typically, course syllabi specify the assignments students are expected to complete during the semester and the dates each of those assignments are due. An alternative is to offer students the option of flexible due dates, using a process that might look like this:

» At the beginning of the semester, students are provided with a list of the assigned projects, papers, and presentations to be completed.
» Instead of providing specific due dates for each assignment, the instructor provides a series of completion dates (e.g., completion date #1, completion date #2).
» Students choose the order in which they complete the assigned tasks for the semester and are merely required to submit one completed assignment on each of the designated completion dates.

This strategy provides students with an opportunity to make decisions about which assignments they can finish first and which assignments will require the greatest amount of time to complete. Additionally, this strategy provides an opportunity to front load assignments and prevents the common practice of requiring a massive amount of completed work during the final two weeks of the semester.

Planning a Sequence of Learning Experiences

Now that we have established the learning outcomes for the first-year seminar and determined the quantity of content that will be included, the next step is to begin planning the sequence of learning experiences that will be offered to students. There are, of course, many paths that can be taken from the starting line to the final destination. Some of these paths are more efficient than others. A few provide more enriched and diverse experiences based upon what is seen and done along the way. It is the task of the faculty member to help each traveler (i.e., student) with the support, encouragement, and direction necessary to make it to the final destination.

The Physics of Time and Space

Teaching in higher education takes place within a specific framework: assigned rooms, master schedules of course offerings, credit hours, semesters, and clock hours invested in the classroom. Within that framework, faculty members must make a series of instructional decisions dramatically impacted by the physics of teaching, namely time and space.

Time. Once the semester starts, college faculty need to decide what is to be taught and the pace at which content is presented, processed, and learned. At midsemester, a faculty member may lament, I am so far behind I will never be able to catch up. This frequently made comment contains several assumptions. First, there is a specified body of knowledge that must be delivered to students enrolled in the course. Further, the pace at which information is shared is slower than anticipated, and to make up the difference, the instructor needs to talk faster and move more quickly through the course content. Finally, such a statement assumes covering the material is the highest, most important, and most noble instructional outcome.

Similarly, the individual class session may make poor use of the time allotted to cover a topic, leading to frustration for students. We have probably all experienced this in our professional lives, perhaps attending a presentation by a well-known expert in a field about which we know very little. The session, although filled with valuable informational tidbits, has not been very well planned. As time runs out, the presenter laments there is much more information that needs to be covered, but time will not permit it. The presenter agrees to provide a copy of the PowerPoint slides. While a nice gesture, the slides likely do not adequately capture the information, which would have been reviewed and illuminated in the presentation.

Both examples point to the necessity for good planning. Far too many classes are taught in the absence of a schedule for the semester. Yet, the amount of classroom time available to teach each and every college class, over the span of a semester, is always a known fact. To make the best use of that time, faculty members should ask several key questions: (a) What is the content I actually need to teach my students this semester in this particular course? (b) What is the process I will use to determine, narrow, and verify the content most important and critical for this course? (c) Based upon this inventory of knowledge, skills, and dispositions (i.e., learning outcomes for the course), what are some things I may need to leave out of this course or ask students to pursue outside of class time? (d) How will I apportion the time available? and (e) What are the strategies I will use to reapportion the time available in response to schedule changes and student learning patterns?

Using their responses to these questions, faculty members can create a game plan summarizing the content that will be covered during each of the scheduled classes prior to the beginning of every course and every semester. For planning purposes, this tentative schedule can simply be a listing of topics, learning outcomes, assigned readings, and assignments that are due, but it can still be shared with students. By providing students with a schedule for each class describing the learning outcomes, topics to be discussed, assigned readings, and any assignments and activities that may be part of the day's learning, faculty members communicate their interest in the class, the students, and the course curriculum. As a caveat, unexpected delays, changes, and other factors may impact the schedule that has been designed; however, these occurrences should be considered an exception rather than a rule. Once the general schedule has been developed, instructors can design an agenda for each class session. Two strategies for developing a class agenda—The Bookshelf and The Rule of Ten and Two—are described in greater detail below.

» *The Bookshelf Strategy* (Smith et al., 2005) intermingles times of lecture and demonstration with thoughtfully designed activities and discussion questions that encourage students to think at a deeper level and begin connecting the dots between this class session (and the associated readings and assignments) and the larger picture of the course content.

- As a starting point, we can visualize a collection of assorted texts arranged on a bookshelf. They cover an assortment of topics and have been written in varied formats depending on the intentions of the author. Instructional planning is the process of arranging these books in a coherent and thoughtful manner.

- The first volume we select from the bookshelf, and the beginning of our classroom teaching session, is an advance organizer. This activity (e.g., an outline of key topics, a fill-in-the-blank outline of the day's learning experiences, an agenda, a partial copy of PowerPoint slides, an introductory video clip, a provocative question, a reference to a current global event that connects with the topic of the day) sets the tone for and introduces the focus of the day's learning experiences. This is a critically important step in the instructional process. By outlining the major topics or outcomes for the day, faculty members are preparing students for what lies ahead. From the perspective of cognitive psychology, instructors who use advance organizers are also creating a structure that will allow students to establish a context for the day's learning experiences and means to organize their thinking.

- The next volume on the bookshelf is a 10-12 minute lecture, video, or demonstration focused on the learning outcomes for the day. This segment is like a mini class, a highly organized, brief activity that communicates one or two specific points. While the content should be presented in a manner allowing this portion of the class to stand alone, each lecture or demonstration segment needs to connect with one another and the overall learning outcomes for the day. We might think of these lecture and demonstration segments as pieces of a puzzle that come together to form a larger picture.

- Volume 3 is a three- to five-minute learning activity specifically designed to assist students in processing the information from the preceding mini lesson through guided discussion in small groups or with a learning partner. Successful guided discussion periods depend on good questions, which Bain (2004) also suggests are a key element in learning and the development of critical thinking skills. He also identifies two parts to the questioning process: (a) designing an intriguing question and (b) helping students understand the significance of the question. Asking good questions—which invite differences of opinion, controversy, and deep thinking—is an art form. For example, if the topic of conversation was a news story involving a special interest group supporting required recycling, students could be asked to make arguments on both sides of the issue. The discussion might culminate in a vote on the issue.

- Subsequent volumes on the bookshelf are interchanged periods of lecture, video, or demonstration and guided discussion.

- The final volume we select from the shelf, is a cohesion builder (e.g., application activity, simulation, problem-based learning activity) designed to help students bring together the key points of the day's class and summarize their newly acquired knowledge, skills, and dispositions. Returning to the analogy of the three boxes from earlier in the chapter, the cohesion builder is the process of taking the box full of content and topping it with a big red bow. The goal of the cohesion builder is to equip students with three or four talking points that summarize the key content and ideas of the class session.

» *The Rule of Ten and Two* is a useful guideline for establishing the relationship between teacher talk and student processing (Garmston & Wellman, 1999, 2002). Simply put, faculty should commit that for every 10 minutes of information sharing (e.g., lecture, video, reading), students should be given a minimum of two minutes to process the knowledge and facts being considered. This can be accomplished through a variety of group-learning experiences readily available in the professional literature, on the Internet, and through campus-based faculty development resources (see appendix). This instructional guideline often creates a challenge for college faculty members, as most have the tendency to revert to talking as a means of filling the available time rather than relying on the power of silence (i.e., the awkward time between the asking of a question and the time that someone is willing to offer a response). To assess adherence to the Rule of Ten and Two, instructors can track the amount of time they spend talking during a class session as compared to the talking time offered to students.

Space. There are a wide variety of classroom configurations and architectural styles represented on college campuses: lecture halls with sloped floors and fixed seating, rooms with movable furniture, rooms with tables and chairs, conference rooms, and so on. It is interesting to note that the seating styles found in academic buildings can generally be traced to the time when these buildings were constructed (e.g., buildings from the 1970s feature large lecture halls with sloped floors, buildings built after the year 2000 feature movable tables and chairs). As Bligh (2000) observes, the architectural style of the classroom reflects certain beliefs about faculty, students, teaching, and learning:

> With pride architects build terraced lecture halls in colleges and universities equipped with the best projection facilities. They represent a conception of education in which teachers who know give knowledge to students who do not and are therefore supposed to have nothing worth contributing. (p. 3)

The architecture of a classroom can dramatically impact the choice of instructional strategies and even the range of options seemingly available. For example, in a classroom with sloped floors and fixed seating, it is generally difficult to use interactive or small-group learning strategies. Although it is possible to ask students in these settings to engage in dialogue with their neighbor or those seated around them, large-group lecture settings generally encourage participants to, at best, face forward and passively watch the speaker or PowerPoint projection screen. As a counterpoint, for faculty who are inclined to lecture, a classroom where students are seated around tables facing different directions can be a distraction and an invitation for inattention. Space is a challenge that must be addressed in pursuit of the most favorable learning conditions.

Connecting Points

When faculty members sign on to teach a first-year seminar, it involves a commitment to design a specified number of hours of classroom instruction as well as associated readings and assignments. There is no substitute for effective planning, which includes looking at the big picture of the first-year seminar (i.e., what do we plan to accomplish over the entire course) in relation to the learning experiences that will be undertaken as part of each class session. This process begins with the identification of learning outcomes or objectives that describe what students should be able to do or know as a direct result of participating in this course.

Development of the course syllabus is a key aspect of success in the first-year seminar. There are, however, many varied ways to design and present the syllabus. This chapter provides faculty with a roadmap for accomplishing the journey that will be traveled over the course of a semester. Although the syllabus cannot answer every possible contingency that will occur, it does offer a structure for what is planned for the semester (e.g., learning outcomes, forms of assessment, textbooks, schedule of learning experiences).

Finally, after presenting an overview of the course through the syllabus, it is time to begin creating a range of learning experiences that systematically move students toward accomplishing identified learning outcomes. This requires faculty engage in long-range planning (i.e., from the perspective of the entire semester), and in a more focused basis, as they design learning experiences that will occur within individual classroom sessions. Good teaching requires good planning.

Chapter 4
Special Considerations in Teaching

It's the little details that are vital. Little things make big things happen.
—John Wooden

Throughout this text, an effort has been made to continually communicate the unique and exciting nature of the first-year seminar. A critical part of that process is to create a learning environment in which students can take risks; explore new areas of learning; and grow in their understanding of themselves, others, and course content. In this chapter, we will explore some of the key ingredients leading to accomplishment of those outcomes. We will consider

- » Building community in the classroom, including establishing standards of civility
- » Setting and enforcing attendance policies
- » Selecting and using textbooks
- » Facilitating out-of-class learning
- » Linking the first-year seminar to other classes and campus life

Building Community in the Classroom

On the first day of class, students wait expectantly for the faculty member to arrive. They look around and see a collection of unfamiliar faces. What are they feeling and thinking? Some show their anticipation and sense of anxiety about the coming semester, a few hide those feelings behind laughter and idle conversation, others are preoccupied with a text message or the safety of a laptop computer screen. No one dares tip their hand in the game of classroom charades. A subtle sense of tension fills the room. The door opens and in walks the faculty member who will guide and direct the group's learning over the next 15 weeks. Questions flood the students' minds as they try to gauge how they are feeling in expectation of the first words of wisdom of the semester.

The ceremonial first pitch of any semester is a recitation from the syllabus. In these first few minutes of the course, students begin to wonder about this person who speaks so eloquently about learning outcomes, due dates, and the importance of class attendance. These facts are all very important, yet the students find themselves wondering whether the faculty member is married, has children, has a favorite flavor of ice cream, and the names of his or her favorite books and movies. These questions all cluster around the theme, Who is this person I will listen to and interact with over the next several months?

Secondarily, there is a tendency to unconsciously assess the sense of whether or not this classroom will be a good place to learn—a place where class members can take risks in the learning process, make mistakes without fear of embarrassment, express opinions with the expectation of dialogue rather than reprisal, and ask questions about areas of confusion without hesitation. These elements create a learning environment where participants can flourish and a sense of community synergy begins to emerge.

To begin this process of community building, faculty members must first consider the following questions about the atmosphere, culture, and expectations for their classrooms:

» What would students say about my willingness to engage in dialogue that invites a variety of opposing opinions and perspectives on issues about which I feel strongly?
» Am I willing to listen rather than speak?
» Are there times I have responded to a student's question or comment in a way that was unintentionally hurtful or minimizing? Did I make an effort to reconcile that relationship with a follow-up conversation?
» Is my classroom a place where I take risks in learning and encourage my students to do the same? What are some ways this approach to learning is evidenced?
» When the time comes to talk with a student about a classroom issue (e.g., excessive absences, plagiarism, poor overall performance), do I engage in the conversation in a manner that sends the message of concern while also respecting the student's personal dignity?
» What are some of the other possible indicators and criteria for creating a community-oriented learning space?

McKinney, McKinney, Franiuk, and Schweitzer (2006) examined the level at which it is possible to create a sense of community within a classroom and the factors contributing to the achievement of that goal. Relying on the research from neighborhood and community development studies, six variables are considered critical to establishing a sense of community among groups of individuals: (a) connection, (b) participation, (c) safety, (d) support, (e) belonging, and (f) empowerment. In the classroom setting, these variables were defined in the following way:

» Connection (e.g., promoting the manner in which students get to know one another from the first day of class)
» Participation (e.g., required daily reflections that were considered to be an admission ticket for class)
» Safety (e.g., ongoing opportunities for students to confer with those seated around them and build trust)
» Support (e.g., pairing high-achieving students with those who need additional assistance and tutoring)
» Belonging (e.g., casual, informal conversations before class between the faculty member and the students)
» Empowerment (e.g., encouraging students to ask questions during class)

Faculty participating in this study made intentional efforts to promote the six variables identified as part of the community-building process. Students involved in the study were able to articulate and describe the differences they noted while members of this classroom community. Results revealed the ways in which small, intentional acts by a faculty member, and a thoughtful approach to building community as a goal for the semester, can positively impact student success (i.e., improved class performance, class satisfaction, and perception of learning). For each of us as faculty members, it is important to continually assess the levels at which we are helping students to connect, participate, feel safe, feel supported, belong, and sense their own empowerment.

It would be a mistake to talk about the classroom as a community for learning without invoking the wisdom of Parker Palmer (1999), who offers the following advice on what can emerge as teachers and students collaborate and learn from one another:

The gift we receive on the inner journey is the knowledge that ours is not the only act in town. Not only are there other acts out there, but some of them are even better than ours, at least occasionally! We learn that we need not carry the whole load but that we can share it with others, liberating us and empowering them. We learn that sometimes we are free to lay the load down altogether. The great community asks us to do only what we are able and trust the rest to other hands. (p. 89)

This picture requires we rethink the dynamics of the classroom. Certainly the faculty member carries a major responsibility for creating a safe place for learning and for sharing his or her knowledge in the field of discussion. At the same time, however, the master teacher will create places and opportunities for students to step into a role of leadership, facilitation, and shared responsibility for what happens in the classroom.

Allowing students ownership of the classroom learning environment requires a willingness to engage in risk taking on the part of the instructor and students. For students, an essential part of the learning process is taking risks with new information, passions, and ideas. In a safe learning environment, students feel the freedom to share their dreams, talk about their fears, and propose extreme responses to the circumstances of our world. As teachers, we have the privilege to create learning experiences that help students focus their energies, refine their skills, and learn lessons making the next risk-taking opportunity seem less formidable.

Creating a Civil Learning Environment

For community to thrive in the classroom, instructors and students must work together to create a civil learning environment. While this is frequently a challenging and sensitive question for faculty members, it is critically important we give thought to the types of acceptable behaviors, as well as those that may pose a threat or disruption to the learning process. Most often, the topic is discussed from the perspective of what bothers faculty about the behaviors of students. However, students have decided opinions about what is appropriate in the classroom and, thus, might be productively engaged in setting community standards for civility. Bjorklund and Rehling (2010) surveyed students and asked them to identify behaviors of their peers that they found to be uncivil. The 10 most frequently listed behaviors included (a) continuing to talk after being asked to stop, (b) coming to class under the influence of drugs or alcohol, (c) allowing a cell phone to ring, (d) conversing loudly with others, (e) swearing, (f) nonverbal disrespect, (g) sleeping, (h) making disparaging remarks,

(i) arriving late or leaving early, and (j) sending and receiving text messages. The authors conclude it is incumbent on faculty to identify those behaviors of concern, communicate them to students, and be prepared to enforce standards of behavior as necessary.

Colosimo (2004) suggests a more positive and affirming approach to fostering civility than creating a set of behavioral rules or standards. She suggests faculty embody five basic ideas that promote active student involvement and make them a priority for all classroom participants. These include (a) extending a welcome to students as members of the learning community (i.e., expressing an interest in their lives, knowing students by name), (b) being present in the moment (e.g., focusing attention on the activities of the classroom), (c) listening deeply (e.g., identifying and acknowledging the thoughts and feelings of others), (d) speaking kindly, and (e) guarding time (e.g., punctuality).

Instructors must begin thinking about the expectations they place on students; the reasoning behind those expectations; the manner in which they are communicated; and strategies for enforcing them in a fair, reasonable, and humane manner. The following recommendations offer additional guidance for promoting civility in the classroom:

» *Create a list of civility expectations for the classroom.* The list should include those things a faculty member considers to be most important along with some suggestion of why those items are important and whether he or she is willing to expend the effort necessary to enforce those identified expectations. Completing the Classroom Civility Inventory (Figure 4.1) can serve as a useful first step in developing this list.

» *Confirm the validity and fairness of the list.* Trusted faculty colleagues can provide honest feedback on the behaviors identified.

» *Communicate expectations to students in a variety of ways.* At a minimum, it is necessary to include the list of desired behaviors in the course syllabus and to talk with students about the rationale for these particular behaviors and the role of civility in their current and future lives.

» *Consistently enforce the expectations communicated to students.* Students typically expect and respect fairness in the administration of classroom and school rules. If we set a standard for behavior, we should also be willing to do the hard work of enforcing it.

Place a checkmark by those items on the following list that you believe are inappropriate in your classroom and that you will enforce through your syllabi and classroom procedures:

___ Eating/drinking in class

___ Overtly sleeping in class (i.e., head down or propped up with eyes closed)

___ Using a laptop computer in class for purposes other than taking notes or participating in classroom activities (e.g., electronic games, email, Facebook. Google)

___ Reading a textbook or other material that is unrelated to course content or classroom activities

___ Talking out inappropriately to the extent that it is disruptive to the learning process

___ Arriving late to class

___ Leaving behind trash (e.g., cups, containers, wrappers)

___ Wearing a hat or hood in class

___ Talking with a neighbor during class to the extent that the volume of their voices becomes noticeably disruptive

___ Overt, ongoing demonstrations of affection toward another student

___ Text messaging or other forms of cell phone usage

___ Inappropriate or rude comments to classmates or faculty during class discussions

___ Other (specify) _____

___ Other (specify) _____

Figure 4.1. The classroom civility inventory. Reprinted from *A Brief Guide for Teaching Millennial Learners* by J. B. Garner, 2007, p. 34. Copyright 2007 by Triangle Publishing. Used with permission.

In a 2006 keynote address at the National Conference on Students in Transition, Scott Evenbeck, former University College dean at Indiana University – Purdue University Indianapolis, made the following observation about one of the greatest ironies of higher education practice:

Behavior is a function of the person and the environment. So our entering students come to campus and we expect them to figure out our rules and our assumptions and our way of doing things.... On campus, our philosophy is that students are adults. Children one day and miraculously transformed into adults the next. Really quite amazing.... But, we have this happy fiction that they will be adults who make choices and live with consequences and then will grow up and live happily ever after. (p. 4)

If we are serious about preparing our students for life after college, then we have a responsibility to define the parameters of acceptable behavior (e.g., coming to class, demonstrating appropriate classroom social skills, respect for self and others) and enforce those expectations in a fair, consistent, and reasonable manner. Being serious about civility, although just one more thing we have to do, is a valuable and important contribution faculty members can make to the lives of their students.

Setting and Enforcing Attendance Policies

At first glance, the question of whether attendance should be taken in college classrooms seems to be a no-brainer. It would seem to make perfect sense that a person spending (or borrowing) tens of thousands of dollars per year for the privilege of attending college classes and earning a degree would logically choose to attend class on a regular basis. Further, it would also be logical to assume class attendance dramatically contributes to enhanced levels of learning. Finally, going out on a limb, we might also assume students, faculty members, and administrators would all agree these propositions are reasonable and rational. Yet, nothing could be further from the truth. The flurry of discussion and activity around the issue of classroom attendance polices can be addressed from three different perspectives: (a) political, economic, and cultural arguments; (b) the empirical evidence regarding the value of classroom attendance; and (c) strategies for increasing student attendance patterns.

Political, Economic, and Cultural Arguments

Ironically, or so it would seem, many faculty members, as well as students argue against the logic and necessity of attendance policies. Petress (1996) summarized some of the key arguments posed by these groups:

» Students claim they are adults who should be given the freedom to decide whether or not they attend classes.
» Students also see themselves as customers and call on university officials to ensure the college courses are solid enough to entice regular attendance (i.e., make classes worth attending).

» Faculty members resist the responsibility of making distinctions between excused and unexcused absences.
» Faculty frequently express concern about the procedural burden imposed by implementing a classroom attendance policy.
» Faculty also raise the issue that mandatory attendance policies infringe on their academic freedom.

Issues related to attendance also play out rather dramatically in the worlds of culture and politics. Some universities, for example, have made a decision not to schedule classes on Fridays because those classes typically demonstrate poor attendance patterns. For students, this is a wonderful gift, as it results in an abundance of three-day weekends. Yet, Young (2003) reports many universities are beginning to see the folly in canceling classes on Fridays and are now making efforts to reclaim this important instructional time and insist on a five-day class week.

In the political arena, the former New York City Mayor Rudy Guiliani threatened to take away $110 million dollars in money from the City University of New York because officials failed to enforce classroom attendance policies (Archibold, 1998). From a learning and accountability perspective, Giuliani believed the failure to take attendance sent a negative message about the quality of the classes being offered and the actual value of attendance and participation.

Empirical Evidence Regarding the Value of Attendance Policies

Numerous research studies have been conducted to investigate the relationship between the attendance patterns of college students and their levels of academic achievement and learning (e.g., Clump, Bauer, & Whiteleather, 2003). Some studies have demonstrated that students who attend classes are often those who have the discipline necessary to "take more and more control of their own learning" (VanBlerekom, 2001, p. 488). These are the intrinsically motivated students who not only feel an obligation to attend class but also to complete assigned readings, pursue excellence in assignments, and to accrue as much knowledge as possible from their college education.

One interesting study by Moore (2003) revealed students believe better class attendance is a contributing factor in receiving a higher grade (and hopefully more learning). Ironically, while students felt they should receive credit for attending class, they also wanted their final grade to be based on what they knew rather than class attendance. Students also believed attending class in college is generally less important than attending classes in high school. One reason for this is in high school taking attendance is simply part of the standard operating procedure. Students know teachers take attendance and someone is monitoring their attendance patterns. In college, those patterns of behavior among faculty members are generally less consistent. This lack of consistency may lead students to conclude attendance is less important in college.

Strategies for Increasing Attendance

With increasing concern about attendance has come efforts to develop strategies for encouraging students to attend class. While faculty members may debate whether the carrot or the stick is a better tool for facilitating regular class attendance patterns, a variety of strategies are available to promote attendance, including the following:

» Spending time at the beginning of the semester discussing the value and rationale for the course attendance policy (Moore, 2003)
» Giving in-class quizzes on a regular basis (Thompson, 2002)
» Using exit cards, which require students to respond to a series of summative questions at the end of each class (Davies & Wavering, 1999). Sample questions could include, What was the big idea for today's class? or How might your connect the theories from today's class with others described in your textbook?
» Making classes more engaging and interesting for the students (Gump, 2005)
» Providing, and talking about, incentives and penalties for attendance (e.g., point deductions for class absences, requirements that students make up missed classes by listening to podcasts and the completion of writing assignments, additional points for perfect attendance)

Selecting and Using Textbooks

To be sure, large, heavy textbooks are often considered to be part of the culture of a college campus—the calling card of a scholarly life. Yet, there are a number of faulty assumptions undergirding the use and selection of textbooks and their overall role in the learning process. While instructors should not be dissuaded from selecting a textbook and assigning readings from it in their courses, they should be consciously aware of the following assumptions as they engage in that process.

Assumption 1: Textbooks are produced primarily with student learning in mind. First and foremost, the people who publish and sell textbooks are in the business of generating profit. Their business is totally dependent upon attracting the attention of potential textbook adoptions by college faculty members. This is accomplished by clever marketing, the plentiful availability of examination copies, website resources, and prefabricated test question banks. This observation is not intended to demean the textbook publishing industry; rather, it serves as a reminder to faculty members to be wise and careful consumers and textbook adopters. The latest edition or newest treatment may not represent the best available vehicle for student learning.

Assumption 2: Textbooks should be a vital and integral part of the learning process in the courses we teach. Quite often, courses are designed and offered in deference to the content and organizational structures found in the textbooks chosen by faculty. The sequence of events that typically transpires is

1. Faculty members select a textbook (or textbooks) that provides the best coverage of the topics to be covered in the course.
2. The course schedule is created based upon the sequence of chapters as they appear in the textbook.
3. Lectures and tests are designed in accordance with the sequence of chapters found in the book.

The logical next question becomes whether these decisions about textbook selection impact student learning in the ways we might envision and hope to realize. Faculty are encouraged to critically examine the textbooks they choose and the degree to which they drive student learning experiences in the course rather than the desired learning outcomes.

Assumption 3: Students actually read their textbooks. The research available on the textbook reading habits of college students is remarkably scarce. What is available, however, is rather disturbing. A study by Connor-Greene (2000) revealed 72% of surveyed students never read their assignments by the due date. In another study, Sikorski et al. (2002) found as many as 30% of the students surveyed indicated they did not purchase a text for at least one of their scheduled courses. Clump, Bauer, and Bradley (2004) report many college students spend less than three hours per week reading assigned textbook materials. Faculty should be strongly encouraged to integrate textbook content into their teaching and to select reading materials that amplify course content and take students to deeper levels of knowledge and understanding about the course content.

Assumption 4: The question, Will this be on the test?, is actually an indication of dedication and motivation on the part of the student as learner. Although many students are committed to learning, there is also a sizeable group of students who are interested in doing only what is necessary to pass certain courses. One question to consider, however, is the source of the questions on the test. Do they come from class lectures, the text, or both? Instructors should provide students with guidance as to the most important concepts, skills, and principles to take away from the course. More specifically, they should help students discern what are the key elements and the intended outcomes of reading assignments. These critical concepts and outcomes must then be reflected in the tests or other assignments instructors design for the course.

Assumption 5: There are no other options to consider. We need textbooks in our courses. Textbooks and other reading materials are critically important to the learning process. Through these resources, students not only acquire new information but also learn the important skill of searching and seeking answers to the predominant questions in their field of study. Clearly, textbooks are an easily accessible source of information, but they are not the only valid source for course content. In an era when information changes rapidly, faculty should systematically engage students with other resources including blogs, journals, newspapers, digital presentations from experts around the world, and websites. Part of this process involves making students aware of these venues for learning. A second component, however, is teaching them the skills to discern between credible sources and only marginally accurate ones.

Strategies to Encourage the Reading of Assigned Texts

As noted above, instructors should not be explicitly discouraged from using traditional textbooks in their courses. At the same time, they need to engage in strategies that will encourage students to read textbooks (and other assigned readings) and make better use of those texts in the course. They may also consider possible alternatives to traditional textbooks as a way of ensuring assigned readings support the intended learning outcomes rather than determining what the possible outcomes may be. The strategies below are designed to increase the likelihood students will take advantage of the reading materials included in their courses.

» *Assigning course-related point values to assigned readings.* Surprisingly, and quite often, the expectation that students are actually required to read the assigned text is implied but not specifically stated. Students may, therefore, assume as long as they acquire the necessary material, reading the text is merely an optional experience. By stating course-related points are available for reading the textbook as assigned and in a timely manner, possible misunderstandings are eliminated. At the end of the semester, students are asked to sign a document on which they indicate the number of points (e.g., 80/100) they are entitled to receive. Interestingly, I have observed students downgrading the points they receive, based upon the level of work they have done, even at the cost of earning a lower grade.

» *Using journal article collections as an alternative to published textbooks.* With the advent of electronic databases commonly available in college libraries, it is possible to create a customized, Internet-based reading collection of full-text articles from a variety of journals and authors. This practice provides a means for selecting reading assignments more current than textbooks, offers varied and opposing viewpoints on the topics of discussion, exposes students directly to the work of experts in the field, and provides a means for more in-depth investigations of key course issues. A single textbook cannot generally accomplish all of these outcomes.

» *Ensuring lectures and other classroom learning experiences are only supplements to assigned reading.* Quite often, there is a high degree of overlap between the materials contained in assigned readings and the content of classroom lectures. Students are quick to realize this condition and draw the conclusion that listening in class (and perhaps taking notes) is a more efficient strategy than listening in class and reading the assigned materials. For faculty members, it is a good idea to conduct a periodic check to determine the level of overlap between lectures and readings.

» *Referencing lectures to information and illustrations contained in the course texts.* During classroom discussions and lectures, faculty should make frequent references to the materials covered in assigned textbooks. This strategy provides a coherent and comprehensive picture of course content and subtly reinforces the faculty member's commitment to both sources of learning and information.

» *Resisting the temptation to use PowerPoint slides that mirror the textbook.* Textbook publishers have become very clever in providing additional resources to faculty designed to make textbook adoption and subsequent teaching quick and easy. One of the most common resources is a set of

PowerPoint slides. Unfortunately, those slides are often simply an outline version of the textbook. Students discover very quickly they do not really need to read the book because the PowerPoint slides have done the work of creating a Spark Notes version of the text.

» *Offering occasional open-book tests.* There are times in every class and every discipline when application of course content is more critical than recognition or recall of facts and concepts. At these times, students can be given questions or scenarios to resolve with the information contained in their textbook. A study by Agarwal, Karpicke, Kang, Roediger, and McDermott (2008) revealed students can actually increase their overall levels of retaining information while preparing to participate in open-book tests. In a culture where information is so readily available, there is value to providing students with access to course-related materials and creating examinations focusing on the application of that data to presented scenarios.

» *Giving quizzes on assigned reading materials.* One way of encouraging students to read the assigned course materials (e.g., text chapter, journal article, web-based information) is to schedule accountability procedures during class (e.g., group discussions on reading assignments, quizzes). In our first-year seminar, which is heavily oriented toward a body of academic content, we began requiring students to complete an online quiz each week covering the assigned readings and the content shared in class. The interesting byproduct of this strategy was a dramatic increase in the students' midterm examination grades. Through the use of online quizzes, they were forced to maintain pace with the readings and classroom materials.

» *Providing written study guides that correspond with assigned course readings.* In every course there are key pieces of information, concepts, and facts that are crucial (and often form the core of examinations and evaluation procedures). Study guides provide students with a means for focusing their attention and effort. If a portion of the information contained in the study guide can only be found in the textbook, then students will need to explore and understand that information by using their textbook as a resource.

» *Linking class participation to advanced preparation.* This strategy assumes a prerequisite to informed participation in class discussions is based, at least partially, on the completion of assigned readings. In a Read and Speak strategy, students are asked to sign in for class only if they have completed the assigned readings for the day's class and are prepared to contribute to the class discussion of those readings.

Facilitating Out-of-Class Learning

A recurring dilemma in higher education is how to design and implement the most powerful and productive learning experiences for our students. Rhoads (1997) relates an exchange with a colleague who laments the apathy of the students in his classes, yet Rhoads found these same students to be particularly politically and socially engaged in his own community service work.

> It later occurred to me that perhaps we were talking about two different groups of students. Then, on second thought, I realized we were talking about two different aspects of students' lives: the classroom and the world beyond the classroom. Perhaps where we have failed most in helping students make the connection between academic work and lived experience is that we have too narrowly defined the classroom as that place that has desks, walls, and a teacher. (p. 28)

Kuh, Douglas, Lund, and Ramin-Gyurnek (1994) suggest to expand the boundaries of learning beyond the classroom walls, college faculty should create instructional opportunities that "integrate in-class knowledge with their [students'] out-of-class lives" (p. 79). This recommendation supports the maxim that learning in higher education gains depth and significance based upon the degree to which students are invited to apply, process, personalize, and engage instructional content (Cox & Orehovec, 2007; Spence, 2001). We will address this topic from several perspectives: (a) facilitating informal faculty-student interactions outside the classroom, (b) linking the first-year seminar with other courses, and (c) finding ways to promote students' engagement with the college campus or culture.

Encouraging Informal Interactions With Faculty

Integrative out-of-class learning experiences can include a focus on building and enhancing relationships with faculty as well as enriching content-related knowledge and understanding. In the book *Now and Then: A Memoir of Vocation* by Frederick Buechner (1983) describes his experiences as a seminary student and the lasting impact of many of his teachers:

> In the last analysis, I have always believed, it is not so much their subjects that the great teachers teach as it is themselves.... Though much of what these teachers said remains with me still and has become so much a part of my own way of thinking and speaking that often I sound like them without realizing it, it is they themselves who left the deeper mark. (p. 12)

If Buechner's observations are correct, what are the factors that contribute to being the kind of teacher who leaves a deeper mark in the lives of students? Three basic ingredients include (a) transparency, (b) demonstrating care, and (c) sharing with students. Teachers who are transparent allow their students to see and feel the course content through their own enthusiasm and passion for the materials and strategies they are sharing and using. Second, it is important instructors let students know they care about them as individuals and as learners. Not only do exemplary teachers value acquisition of new and important content material, but they also strongly value students' growth as people.

As a means of organizing our thoughts around the importance of faculty-student interactions, we consider the typology proposed by Cox and Orehovec (2007) who envision a continuum of interactive possibilities ranging from the most removed (and most frequent) to the most involved (and least frequent). These include

» Disengagement (i.e., faculty and students do not interact outside the classroom)
» Incidental contact (i.e., unintentional, perfunctory contact, including polite greetings)
» Functional interaction (i.e., contacts directly related to academic questions, activities, and concerns)
» Personal interaction (i.e., purposeful interactions centering around personal interests of the faculty member and the student)
» Mentoring (i.e., direct assistance with career development, assistance in resolving personal challenges, serving as a role model).

As faculty, it is helpful to periodically take the time to assess the ways we are engaging with our students and the strategies we are employing to making connections and build relationships. The following strategies are suggestions for building faculty-student relationships:

» *Assessing connections between faculty and students.* In our first-year seminar, we have a breakout group component often taught by a variety of faculty and staff members (e.g., student affairs professionals, residential life staff, others from the campus community). One of the informal strategies I employ to assess the level at which faculty and staff are connecting with students is to ask students to name their breakout leader. My theory is students who can name their breakout leader have made personal connections. I do the same with faculty and staff by strongly encouraging them to learn and then use their students' names during class and in out-of-class conversations. Taking the time and effort to learn something about students (e.g., hometown, academic major, favorite sports teams, their participation in campus activities) pays great dividends and demonstrates an interest in their lives.

» *Encouraging informal interactions between faculty and staff.* As part of our first-year seminar, we provide extra credit for students who make arrangements to have coffee or share a meal with faculty members (i.e., either first-year seminar faculty or faculty from other classes they are taking that semester). Yet, students may be uncomfortable taking the initiative to invite an instructor to lunch. One way to help students break the ice and encourage them to interact with first-year seminar faculty is the Hello My Name Is... strategy. Here, instructors encourage students to walk up to them and introduce themselves if they see them on campus or in the community. Such an invitation provides the impetus many students need to make informal contact with a faculty member.

» *Disclosing deeply held beliefs and values to students.* Our personal commitments are central to who we are as people and as teachers. Palmer (1997) suggests an integral part of the process and experience of being a teacher is having the courage to share our lives with our students, both inside and outside of the classroom. We invite them to learn about the values, beliefs, and character traits that are not only a part of our conversations but that also play a central role in determining our actions, decisions, and choices. This level of engagement adds credibility and power to our roles as both teachers and mentors.

Linking the First-Year Seminar to Other Classes

George Kuh, perhaps the leading advocate for the creation of higher education environments that welcome, value, and engage students, has coined the term *involving colleges* to describe schools that "provide environments that seem to encourage student out-of-class learning" (Kuh, Schuh, Whitt, & Associates, 1991, p. 4). At such institutions, "the blending of curricular and out-of-class learning experiences is acknowledged and valued; everyone is held to high, clearly communicated standards; [and they] value undergraduate learning wherever it occurs" (Kuh et al., 1991, p. 4). As we think about the first-year seminar, it too should be a place that welcomes students to the campus and creates a link to out-of-class learning experiences. One of the strategies that colleges and universities use to accomplish the goal of involving their students is the creation of learning communities. Smith, MacGregor, Matthews, and Gabelnick (2004) define a *learning community* as "a variety of curricular approaches that intentionally link or cluster two or more courses, often around an interdisciplinary theme or problem, and enroll a common cohort of students" (p. 20). Two common ways to organize learning communities are the interest group and the linked course format.

Interest groups often focus on topics connected with student preferences or in association with particular academic majors (e.g., The Writings of Edgar Allen Poe, The Film Genre of Science Fiction, Issues in Social Justice, a topic of common interest chosen for particular academic majors). Quite often, in this arrangement, faculty members are also teaching on topics about which they are particularly passionate. This combination of a student's topical interest and the faculty member's passion about the subject can be a powerful way to begin the first semester on campus.

Linking the first-year seminar with a content-based course (e.g., gateway course in a specific discipline), general education course, or skill-based course (e.g., composition, public speaking) (Galles & Olson, 2008) is another way to facilitate student engagement within the context of a learning community. In these scenarios, a cohort of students enroll in two or more courses that share learning outcomes, syllabi, assignments, and other experiences. By definition, these classes are taught by two or more faculty members, often representing differing academic disciplines. The result, it is hoped, is an interdisciplinary experience where faculty actively engage one another in teaching and dialogue that highlights the similarities and differences that exist between disciplines in relation to study in a particular area of exploration.

For example, a first-year seminar class may be paired with an introductory general education composition class. The faculty members assigned to these classes share the teaching load and the enrolled students, and they create a common syllabus that outlines the course learning outcomes, schedule of learning experiences, readings, assignments, and general classroom policies. The discussions, readings, and assignments are planned and implemented by faculty in each of the two courses. In this way, students are part of a learning community that benefits from the diverse perspectives of faculty members from varied disciplines.

Connecting Students With the Campus at Large

One important function of the first-year seminar is to connect students with the culture and milieu of the college and to acquaint students with the variety of social, cultural, and academic resources that can enhance the quality of their overall learning experience. A strategy to facilitate first-year student interactions with the campus at-large, and the resources and activities available, is the Personalized Learning Experience Portfolio. Over the course of the first semester, as part of the first-year seminar, students are asked to accumulate 100 points by attending and participating in a variety of campus events. A selected sample of events is listed on the portfolio in a variety of categories: athletics, music and drama, residence hall, and lecture or demonstrations (and others fitting into the culture and activities of a particular campus). Students earn 20 points for each of the events they attend and must select one activity from each of the categories. This structure forces (i.e., facilitates, encourages, helps) students to move out of their comfort zones and engage with the various activities and opportunities available during their first semester on campus.

Connecting Points

Effective teaching, particularly in the first-year seminar, requires attention to a variety of details. The more time and effort spent in advance thinking about the total picture of the semester and the ways learning experiences can be structured and organized, the greater the benefit for students. Additionally, advance planning reduces the number of surprises that will need attention and resolution over the course of the semester.

The planning process applies most powerfully to expectations related to student performance (e.g., assignments, readings, civility). Giving students intentional access to the information that will help them plan for success during the semester will increase their chances for success.

Chapter 5
Alternative Approaches to Learning

To teach is to learn twice.—Joseph Joubert

If we were to walk down the hallway of any academic building on any college campus anywhere in the world, there is a high probability the most prevalent sound we would hear coming from the classrooms would be the voices of faculty members delivering lectures. Although there may be brief interludes of conversation around the topic at hand, professors' voices would be almost universally the foremost sounds emanating from these classrooms. Were we to glance in the classrooms, we would likely observe looks of passivity and resignation on the faces of the students seated there. Their physical attitudes and facial expressions may reflect a variety of feelings, including fatigue, boredom, disinterest, and/or capitulation to their required physical presence (but conceivably optional mental engagement). The faculty members standing at the front of those classrooms may be uncomfortably aware that students have mentally checked out but may also feel powerless to change the situation.

These observations are supported by data revealing approximately 83% of surveyed higher education faculty identified the lecture as their primary instructional method (Chen, 2002). The proliferation of the lecture is not a new phenomenon in higher education, as Spence (2001) notes,

> For just a moment, assume that time travel is possible. Plop a medieval peasant in a modern dairy farm, and he would recognize nothing but the cows. A physician of the 13th century would run screaming from a modern operating room. Galileo could only gape and mutter touring NASA's Johnson Space Center. Columbus would quake with terror in a nuclear sub. But a 15th century teacher from the University of Paris would feel right at home in a Berkeley classroom. (p. 13)

Spence's amusing view of change over the past 500 years provides a convicting assessment of pedagogy in higher education: The techniques used for teaching in college classrooms have not kept pace with the levels of innovation and discovery that can be documented in other segments of our culture.

To put this observation in context, however, it is important to consider how new faculty members are typically integrated into higher education. Hiring of faculty is generally based upon a prospective faculty member's demonstrated expertise in an academic discipline (i.e., research, publications, professional affiliations, and accomplishments). That certainly makes sense, as we want faculty who are experts in their fields. Wergin (1988), however, asserts higher education may be the only profession for which people are never formally trained. This observation is related to the paucity of experiences higher education faculty are given to prepare them for standing in front of a classroom with the expectation they will be able to teach effectively in their chosen field of expertise. Having knowledge and being able to communicate that knowledge to others in a way promoting learning are two entirely different skill sets. The challenge for faculty members, therefore, is one of staying abreast of the developments in their academic field and continuing to grow and develop as a teacher.

Many opinions, and a considerable amount of rhetoric, have been put forth as possible responses and solutions to this challenge (Barr & Tagg, 1995; Bligh, 2000; Burgan, 2006; Spence, 2001; Tagg, 2003). While the second chapter in this volume described basic principles of effective educational experiences, the remainder of this text will suggest specific strategies for more actively engaging students in the classroom.

Defining the Dimensions of Active Learning

In the annals of higher education, a term that has taken on a variety of meanings is *active learning*, often attributed to the seminal work of John Dewey (1937). To begin our examination of instructional strategies, we will explore some of the parameters for this type of learning as reflected in the professional literature. We will consider the term active learning to be the umbrella under which we will also find other closely related types of pedagogy: cooperative learning, problem-based learning, and service-learning. As you will see, these strategies lend themselves well to the first-year seminar as they provide opportunities for students to engage with one another and the topics of discussion in an intentional and interactive manner.

Bonwell and Eisen (1991) propose that active-learning strategies in higher education classrooms share the following characteristics:

» Involvement as more than listening
» Less emphasis on transmitting information and more on developing students' skills
» Involvement in higher-order thinking (e.g., analysis, synthesis, evaluation)
» Engagement in activities (e.g., reading, discussion, writing)
» Emphasis on students' exploration of their own attitudes and values (p. 2)

This definition of active learning clearly echoes the earlier exploration of the basic principles of effective teaching (i.e., Chickering and Gamson's Seven Principles, Barr and Tagg's Learning Paradigm, and Edgerton's Pedagogies of Engagement) in chapter 2. The definition of active learning also suggests a continuing theme of learning in the company of others, an important emphasis in many first-year seminars. As students enter college, coming from a variety of academic, social, cultural, economic, and ideological backgrounds, it will be helpful and constructive to provide guided experiences that assist them in clarifying their own perspectives while also engaging the perspectives of others. Active learning acknowledges the importance of helping students look beyond their own vantage point through critical thinking, dialogues, explorations, and reflection. These experiences drive learning deeper than a mere accumulation of facts, figures, and intellectual data points.

Models of Active Learning

Reminiscent of the learning paradigm described in chapter 2, Weimer (2002) describes an environment in which learner-centered teaching occurs. For this type of teaching to transpire, she believes five key changes must occur in higher education classrooms:

1. *Balance of power.* In the learning-centered paradigm, faculty become more than simple dispensers of knowledge (i.e., what is often delineated as the difference between the sage on the stage and the guide on the side). Invoking the work of Freire (1974) and the teaching of critical pedagogy, Weimer proposes a setting in which power is shared between teacher and student.

2. *The function of content.* Rather than treating content as an end in itself (i.e., he or she who gathers the most information wins), it can become a vehicle for personal transformation and the gaining of new insights.

3. *The role of the teacher.* The learning-centered teacher serves as a guide and facilitator helping students challenge their sense of absolute knowing (Baxter Magolda, 2000).

4. *The responsibility for learning.* As part of this rethinking of the teaching and learning paradigm, students are given greater levels of responsibility for their own learning. Weimer (2002) eloquently describes this process:

> In general, our instructional policies and practices do not make students thirsty. Rather, we tell students that they are thirsty — that they should be drinking. They remain unconvinced and so (mostly out of concern for them), we force the issue. We use rules, requirements, and sticks to try to hold their heads in the watering trough. Most do end up drinking, but a lot of them never figure out why water is so important. A few drown in the process. (p. 103)

This provision requires faculty to rethink the level at which learning becomes a process of jumping through hoops in order to meet the criteria established by the faculty member as opposed to acquiring new understanding and perspective on the topics included in course content.

5. *Evaluation purposes and processes.* Weimer (2002) admonishes faculty to create assessment strategies that are formative rather than summative (i.e., assessment strategies that help students learn along the way rather than waiting until the final examination, or the paper they hand in the last day of class, to determine what they have learned).

Dale's (1946) Cone of Learning identified a variety of learning techniques and arranged them in order (bottom to top) from the most effective to the least effective (i.e., direct-purposeful experiences, contrived experiences, dramatized experiences, demonstrations, field trips, exhibits, television, motion pictures, recordings, radio, still pictures, visual symbols, verbal symbols). Subsequent to this work, percentages were added to indicate the level at which students are able to typically retain information in response to particular teaching strategies (i.e., teaching others, 90%; practice by doing, 75%; discussion group, 50%; demonstration, 30%; audio-visual, 20%; reading, 10%; lecture, 5%). Despite this apparent precision, no research base has been discovered to substantiate these numbers (Lalley & Miller, 2007).

While there is little empirical evidence to support the Pyramid of Learning (as Dale's Cone of Learning is now often referred to), intuitively it makes good sense. We can all remember a time when we have discovered a passage or a relevant real-world example illustrating a critically important concept in a way that has enhanced our understanding. We want to share the example with students later in the semester and, so, we highlight the text and make comments in the margin describing how and when to use it. Yet, the example remains buried within the pages of the book or in a computer file—highlighted, commented upon, but never used. Alternately, if we use that illustration, once or perhaps more than once, it becomes an integral part of our teaching repertoire. Surely, we all forget things that seem important at the moment we hear them. What makes the difference, intuitively and in accordance with Dale's work, is actually using the newly gained information in a meaningful fashion. That process of use leads to enhanced levels of retention and understanding. As instructors, we need to find ways for students to use new information in significant and meaningful ways.

Another concept often associated with active learning is the process of *experiential learning*. Kolb's (1984) model of experiential learning finds its basis in the work of well-known theorists in the field of education, including Jean Piaget, John Dewey, and Kurt Lewin. The elements of Kolb's model include the learner's (a) participation in concrete experiences, (b) observations and reflections about the experiences, (c) creation of abstract concepts, and (d) tests of those concepts in new situations. Kolb's cyclical model allows learners to experience a constant building of reflective thought and action. Active experimentation in new situations encourages students to apply previously learned concepts, thus leading to reflective observation, changes and additions to previous knowledge, and plans for application of this new knowledge (Merriam & Caffarella, 1999). In the first-year seminar, this could include discussions of controversial topics and current events, provocative speakers, service-learning experiences, or challenging readings with a provision for a written response. Kolb identified four specific types of skills or abilities required of learners for maximum achievement using experiential learning, which include (a) an openness and willingness to involve oneself in new experiences, (b) observational and reflective skills, (c) analytical abilities, and (d) decision-making and problem-solving skills (Merriam & Caffarella, 1999).

These theoretical perspectives on learning all focus on the student's experiences and the ways in which those experiences are translated into concepts, actions, insights, and applications. Eyler (2009) clarifies the purposes and goals for incorporating the practices of experiential learning as an integral part of the curriculum. These include enhancing the student's understanding and appreciation for subject matter, ability to think more deeply about meaning and application of content, and creation of connections with content and concepts from other disciplines. In the first-year seminar, students will be processing many new experiences and working to make sense of college life, new relationships, challenges to things they have always believed, and determining the level at which old strategies for decision making and living apply to new and unique situations.

Cooperative Learning

We will now turn our attention to some strategies that can be used to implement active learning in the first-year seminar. The first general category we will explore is cooperative learning. This set of learning tools draws heavily on research illustrating and supporting the principle that students learn more effectively—and retain information more efficiently—when they are provided with opportunities to discuss, debate, sort out, examine, evaluate, and apply the content knowledge they are gaining through classroom lectures and assigned reading. Spencer Kagan (1994), a key force in the development of the cooperative learning paradigm, suggests there are several key components that must be considered in the design and implementation of this type of instructional experience, including

- » The creation of working teams
- » An environment that promotes cooperation among participating students
- » The faculty member's ability to manage multiple groups working separately on common tasks
- » The facilitation of appropriate social skills (e.g., communication, conflict resolution, listening)
- » Positive interdependence among individual group members
- » Individual accountability for involvement in the process
- » Equal participation
- » Simultaneous interaction
- » Maximized efforts to create positive and productive outcomes

The evidence consistently points to the effectiveness of cooperative learning as a teaching strategy when compared to requiring students to learn on their own (Johnson & Johnson, 1993, 1998a, 1998b; Pascarella & Terenzini, 2005). If these data are so convincing, then why do faculty persist in relying on the lecture as a primary means of instruction? Perhaps, faculty use this method less often because facilitating group work demands a unique skill set or because of the perceived messiness of several small groups of students working side-by-side in a classroom setting. To assist instructors in moving toward this goal in the first-year seminar, we will examine four aspects of facilitating cooperative learning that are critically important: (a) forming groups, (b) monitoring group process, (c) designing group tasks, and (d) evaluating group performance.

Forming Groups

It is customary for students to enter class on the first day, find a seat, and then sit in that same location for the remainder of the semester. This practice necessarily limits their interactions to other students who have chosen seats in their general proximity. To mix things up, and to make the entire first-year seminar experience one where students are always expanding their comfort zone, instructors might use any one of a number of strategies to form small groups as a means of facilitating cooperative group work:

» *Round the clock learning partners* (Garmston & Wellman, 2002). At the beginning of the semester, students are presented with a line drawing of a clock face with 12 hours marked. They are asked to make appointments with 12 different classmates corresponding with each hour on the clock (i.e., a 1:00 partner, a 2:00 partner). As they arrive for class in subsequent weeks, they are asked to sit with a designated partner.

» *Seasonal learning partners* (Garmston & Wellman, 2002). In smaller classes, the *round the clock* strategy can be applied with one minor modification. The students are given a paper with the four seasons of the year. They make appointments with four other people corresponding to the seasons of the year.

» *A sweet way to create groups.* As students arrive for class, they are asked to choose their favorite candy bar from a large bowl of miniatures (e.g., Snickers, Butterfinger, Milky Way). Students are then given the direction to create groups of four with the condition that each group must include members representing four different candy bar brands. Alternatively, you could suggest students form a group of four with people who share their taste in candy bars (i.e., same choices).

» *Count off.* A common way of dividing a class into small groups is to ask the students to count off by fours, fives, sixes, and so forth.

» *What is the deal?* Playing cards are distributed to students randomly. Students are then given the direction to form groups based upon the card they have been dealt (e.g., fours together, queens together). Group sizes can be managed by determining the number of cards for any given designation (i.e., 2s, 3s, 4s) dealt out to the students.

» *My new BFF.* To encourage a more diverse mix of dialogue and opinion, students can stand, look around the room, and identify a person with whom they have not worked or spoken with extensively over the course of the semester. After finding their new BFF (i.e., Best Friend Forever), one student from the pair moves to the other's seating location. The students, then, introduce themselves and shake hands.

Mixing up the ways in which student groups are formed adds some excitement and uncertainty to the learning process.

Monitoring Group Process

After students have been organized into small groups, it is important to remember the process requires monitoring and management. The faculty member assumes the role of facilitator, guide, encourager, and coach, moving around among the groups as they work, randomly sitting down with a group to briefly participate or eavesdrop on their conversation. This simple action communicates that the group process is a vital part of the learning experience in the class. Some strategies instructors can use to facilitate the process and manage the overall level of activity are described below.

» *Time as a variable.* When students participate in group activities, it is often difficult for faculty members to accurately estimate the amount of classroom time appropriate for completing assigned tasks (Garmston & Wellman, 2002). Some groups finish before others, and sometimes, we simply miscalculate the amount of time it will take for groups to organize themselves and work together toward a common goal.

» *Minute fingers* (Garmston & Wellman, 2002). When the allotted time expires and some of the groups have finished while others are still working, instructors can use the minute fingers technique. Groups that are still working can quickly discuss how many additional minutes they will need (between 1 and 5) and then designate one person as their spokesperson.

That person will raise a hand with the corresponding number of fingers extended to designate additional minutes needed. Once all groups have been surveyed, the instructor can announce an average that meets the additional time needed for the groups in the class.

» *The fickle finger of fate.* When students work in groups, there is often a need to designate specific individuals to fulfill varied roles. One way to facilitate this process is to bring the fickle finger of fate into play (Garmston & Wellman, 2002). After students are in groups, class members are asked to raise their right hand with the index finger extended. On the count of three, they are directed to point to the person in their group whom they feel would be the best possible recorder for the group's discussion. That person inherits the role of recorder. As a way of adding a positive spin to being designated as the recorder, that individual is given the privilege of choosing the person in the group who will serve as spokesperson.

We often assume students can spontaneously come together and work as a group accomplishing the tasks laid before them. Yet, a number of things may happen to derail successful group functioning (e.g., a group member who talks incessantly, unshared feelings, ignored frustrations, excessive amounts of time spent on tasks unrelated to the group's mission). Hård af Segerstad, Helgesson, Ringborg, and Svedin's work (as cited in Postholm, 2008) proposes time should be spent in class processing the work that occurs in groups and encouraging some discussion about group norms and rules of operation. During the initial part of a semester, or as groups are first created, it is important to spend some time talking with students about the ways in which groups operate and the challenges that can make groups dysfunctional. For example, as groups begin to organize themselves, students should be encouraged to consider ground rules governing

» Time and location of group meetings
» Expected levels of preparation for meetings
» Discussion, such as
  • Group members who talk too much should learn to be more reticent, and those who say too little should be more active.
  • Each member should state reasons for his or her opinions and way of thinking.
  • It is better for a group member to say he or she does not understand something than to drop out of the discussion.
» Personal responsibility for learning

Time spent on these basic issues early in the group formation process will often prevent the occurrence of disruptive events as the group begins to deal with the tasks at hand.

Group Tasks

There are a variety of tasks that can be configured into group work. As faculty members, we need to continually ask ourselves, Is there a way I can take this content and convert it into a format allowing students to make their own discoveries and develop their own insights? Far too often, we take the easy way out by developing 10 extra PowerPoint slides to communicate the information at hand. Bonwell and Eisen (1991) suggest a variety of ways in which cooperative learning can be integrated into the process of teaching: demonstrations, in-class reflective writing and sharing, debates, and drama. Other ideas for encouraging students to work collaboratively with their classmates include

» *Picture this or sing it.* As a way of capitalizing on the multiple intelligences in the classroom, students are assigned to small groups and asked to capture the major aspects of a concept or body of information in varied formats, including a poster, poem, rap song, television commercial, news interview, on-the-street interview, human sculpture, or a poster depicting a concept without using words.

» *The Cinquain.* A great and often unexpected way of helping students to process and summarize newly acquired knowledge and skills is to encourage them to write poetry. One quick and easy type of poetry students typically enjoy is the cinquain, a five-line poem written in a specific format:

- Line 1: A title of one word or one subject
- Line 2: Two words about the subject
- Line 3: Three verbs that signify action
- Line 4: Four words describing your feelings for line one (words or phrase)
- Line 5: A synonym for line 1

» *Gone in 60 seconds.* Students experience any number of changes as they move through a semester: new insights and learning, new relationships, and the clarification of life goals. Given these potential transformations, it is always helpful to provide opportunities for structured reflection. The Gone in 60 Seconds strategy provides an opportunity for students in a first-year seminar to quickly reflect on and share their learning experience. It can also be adapted for a variety of purposes and academic disciplines. Students are randomly paired and stand facing their partners. A series of questions or prompts are flashed on the classroom screen at 60-second intervals. Students have one minute to consider the statement and share their responses with one another. Interval times can be adjusted accordingly if a question generates a higher level of conversation. Examples of prompts used during a final session of a first-year seminar include

- My biggest surprise during my first semester in college was...
- My biggest success and my greatest disappointment were...
- Three things I have learned about myself are...
- One thing I will do differently next semester is...

» *Something I heard.* As a teacher, it is always encouraging to hear the indescribable buzz that fills a room when students are talking, sharing, and creating in small groups. Quite often, this results in an enhanced level of enthusiasm and excitement on the part of the faculty member. In this heightened state of euphoria, the faculty member reconvenes the large group and asks the fatal question, "Who would like to share some of the ideas and thoughts that were generated in your small group?" Quite often, this invitation results in deafening silence since students are generally reluctant to take the bold step of sharing their ideas with the large group. As a way of circumventing this dilemma, the instructor might ask students to share a thought, idea, or concept that they heard from another member of their group. This approach is much more likely to work as the bright ideas being shared are those of a fellow group member or the group as a whole.

Evaluating Group Performance

As in most group efforts (e.g., committees, teams, task forces), some disparity exists between the level of effort expended and contributions of individual group members in relation to the final product. After one first-year seminar class activity where students were working in groups, I received several angry student e-mails (e.g., I don't like working in groups like this. There are people in our group who are not contributing. This is totally unfair.). I finally had to make a class announcement with a basic message: Get over it. The point here being, for the remainder of their lives, students will be working in groups.

Whether those groups are at work, at church, or in the community, students will be involved in groups where some members will do a high volume of work and others will do very little. What they need to develop as group members are the skills necessary to maximize overall group performance so the final product is their best possible work, regardless of individual contributions.

Yet, faculty members are still left with the difficult task of evaluating group work. Several perspectives can guide assessment of group performance. First, and most obvious, is the final product. What is the overall quality of the work done by the group, and to what extent does this product meet the stated outcomes and expectations? That is often the easiest part of the process and can be tied to a rubric delineating guidelines for success. Underlying that final product, however, is the actual group process of combining abilities, efforts, interests, and motivations (often at vastly different levels) for a final product to emerge. The formative aspects of group performance can be assessed in several ways:

» Groups can be asked to submit weekly minutes of their meetings. These minutes reflect who was in attendance, assignments that have been made for individual group members, and the level at which those tasks have been completed. As a faculty member, it is important to review these group meeting minutes regularly and intervene when it is apparent certain groups are having difficulty working toward the common goal of completing the assignment.

» At the end of the project, students can be asked to use a rubric to evaluate their own and other group members' performance in the areas of preparation, participation, and leadership. This assessment can contribute to a portion of the final grade for the group's efforts. Including this provision in the overall design of cooperative learning communicates the importance of the *process* in moving toward the final *product*.

» One variation on the assignment of points for the performance or contributions of individual group members is to create a system for point distribution. Under this plan, as students are asked to evaluate individual group members' participation in the group (including their own), they are given 50 points to distribute among all of the group members (including themselves) with the idea those receiving the greatest number of points made the greatest contributions to the work of the group.

A final consideration in evaluating group performance is the option for the group to fire a member of their group. On occasion, there are group members who simply disassociate themselves from the work of the group and decide to coast through the process and gather their grade at the end of the effort. The fact this option exists should be shared at the beginning of the assignment along with the necessary prerequisites for considering such a drastic step (e.g., consistently missing group meetings, not completing assigned tasks, extreme interpersonal challenges). If a group member is fired, he or she is then required to submit the entire assignment individually, based upon his or her own efforts. This is a serious decision and one that should not be taken lightly. As a final note, students learn a great deal from intragroup conflicts if they can be healed or solved through faculty-guided conversations.

Final Thoughts on Cooperative Learning

Learning and performing in groups is a vital life skill. Students have the opportunity to acquire new knowledge and talents, while also enhancing their ability to work cooperatively with others—a combination that can have longstanding impact. The facilitation of cooperative learning is a unique skill set and one not many faculty members have acquired during their experiences in higher education. For faculty attracted to this type of learning, and who do not know exactly where to start, the best advice is to find colleagues experienced in this area who can serve as a mentor, guiding their learning and experimentation.

Problem-Based Learning

Problem-based learning (PBL) is a strategy receiving increased attention in higher education. Its origins are often attributed to Thomas Corts of McMaster University in Canada who developed this technique as way of teaching medical education students to create solutions to diagnostic challenges (Rheem, 1998). PBL has been applied to a number of different academic topics, including business (Pennell & Miles, 2009), medicine (Uba, 2009), biotechnology (Marklin Reynolds, & Hancock, 2010), geography (Dittmer, 2010), and poverty (Gardner, Tuchman, & Hawkins, 2010). Duch, Groh, and Allen (2001) provide a description of the PBL process:

In the problem-based learning approach, complex, real-world problems are used to motivate students to identify and research the concepts and principles they need to know to work through these problems. Students work in small learning teams, bring together collective skill at acquiring, communicating, and integrating information. (p. 6)

PBL provides an excellent mechanism for assisting first-year students in gaining and practicing skills that will serve them well throughout their higher education experience and beyond, such as critical thinking, verbal and written communication, team work, and problem-solving skills. It also helps students contextualize the acquisition of new knowledge and skills. Typical phases of the PBL process include (a) presenting the problem, (b) clarifying the questions involved in the problem and generating possible hypotheses, (c) gathering information related to the problem (typically done with team members investigating various components of the issue), (d) reporting back to the group and synthesizing the derived data, and (e) creating the group's response and action plan.

Dolmans, De Grave, Wolfhagen, & van der Vleuten (2005) balance their praise of PBL with a caution about the level of sophistication and planning necessary to effectively develop and facilitate it. Challenges include scenarios that are too tightly defined (i.e., the solution is created without any level of effort), those too loosely defined (i.e., the number of possible solutions is so large or variable that critical analysis becomes a challenge), and problems related to working in a group in pursuit of a collaborative solution. Duch (2001) delineates the qualities of a high-quality PBL scenario:

» The topic of concern should be one that captures the attention and interest of participating students.

» Topics should require students to make judgments and decisions as they uncover relevant options and possible solutions. This process requires participants to analyze a variety of options to choose the best course of action.

» The proposed problem needs to have a level of complexity that requires teams to use all members of the team in the data gathering and decision-making phases.

» Questions should be open-ended to the extent they invite group members to participate.

» There should be a direct connection between the PBL scenario and course learning outcomes.

To understand this process, it may be helpful to examine a sample PBL scenario. One of the discussions we have during our first-year seminar is the process students use to determine their movie-viewing habits. On our campus, a faith-based institution, we have established guidelines that prohibit students from watching movies with an R or NC-17 rating. Exceptions to this policy occasionally can be made by a standing committee comprised of students and faculty members. As you might imagine, this policy draws a considerable amount of discussion and concern from our students (e.g., We are adults. We should be able to make our own decisions.). Regardless of how any of us might feel about this policy, it creates a wonderful opportunity for a relevant and engaging problem-based learning experience. Students are placed into groups of four with the assignment to create a movie-viewing policy for our campus. The process has resulted in some very lively discussions and a wide variety of movie-viewing policies.

After the policies have been drafted, a follow-up evaluation activity helps students to assess the implications of their movie policy. They exchange policies with another group and are asked to complete two tasks: (a) assess the general usability of the policy employing a rubric developed for this purpose and (b) apply the movie policy they are reviewing to three recently released movies. As part of this review process, students provide written comments to the original authors. Examples of ways in which PBL can be applied to a variety of academic disciplines is provided in Figure 5.1.

Other PBL Strategies

PBL activities may be subject to some of the same group process challenges as other cooperative learning activities. Thus, before embarking on a full-scale PBL experience, it is sometimes helpful to engage students in preliminary learning activities that allow them to strengthen their skills in group collaboration, critical thinking, and verbal and written communication. *Jigsaw* and *graffiti* are two strategies that can be implemented within one class session to give students practice with these skills.

Jigsaw. A jigsaw puzzle is a collection of many separate yet connected pieces of information. When assembled in the correct order and orientation, these pieces create a larger picture more complete than any of the component parts are able to depict on their own (Aronson, Stephan, Sikes, Blaney, & Snapp, 1978). In the jigsaw strategy, individual group members become experts in one

- *Life and death decisions in a case of Amyotrophic Lateral Sclerosis*— A man wishes to end his life so that he can donate his organs to others and not suffer the agonizing effects of Lou Gehrig's disease (Political Science, Natural Sciences, Business, Philosophy).
- *Creation or Evolution?*— How should the Adamsville Board of Education decide on guidelines for adopting new textbooks for the local schools? (Education, Philosophy, Natural Sciences, Religion).
- *Storing Hazardous Wastes*—Clintonville is presented with the opportunity to create a hazardous waste storage facility. It will bring tremendous amounts of money into the city's coffers but also presents a serious health risk for city residents (Natural Sciences, Political Science).
- *Fast Food in the School Cafeteria* — School officials are debating the options of serving healthy food in the school cafeteria, which students may refuse to buy, or entering into an agreement with a fast food restaurant, which will result in significant profits for the chain and income for the school (Business, Education, Marketing).
- *Banning Facebook*— University officials are considering the possibility of banning Facebook on campus in favor of a locally sponsored and monitored social media network (First-year seminar, Communications).
- *Shakespeare Lives!*— Students are given the task of reworking the plot of a Shakespearean play into a 21st century scenario (English Composition, World Literature, World History).

Figure 5.1. Sample problem-based learning topics. Reprinted from "Problem-Based Learning: A Strategy for Enhancing the Relevance Connection," by J. B. Garner, 2010, *The ToolBox, 9*(1), 2. Copyright 2010 by the University of South Carolina. Used with permission.

aspect of the problem the group is charged to address or resolve. The jigsaw approach accrues a number of advantages with respect to student learning:

> First and foremost, it is a remarkably efficient way to learn the material. But even more important, the jigsaw process encourages listening, engagement, and empathy by giving each member of the group an essential part to play in the academic activity. Group members must work together as a team to accomplish a common goal; each person depends on all the others. No

one student can succeed completely unless everyone works well together as a team. This "cooperation by design" facilitates interaction among all students in the class, leading them to value each other as contributors to their common task. (Aronson, n.d., para. 6)

It may also provide a useful framework for exploring a variety of thought-provoking and controversial topics that are sometimes incorporated into the first-year seminar (e.g., Should the university monitor student entries on Facebook? or How should we respond to racist comments?). Engagement with these topics goes well beyond simply becoming knowledgeable about a particular area of content. Students also learn skills related to perspective taking and dealing with conflicting points of view. Figure 5.2 offers an example of how this might work in the classroom.

Graffiti. This strategy encourages groups of students to share their ideas in response to a problem or scenario and respond to the ideas generated by other student groups within the class. The technique is easily implemented in the college classroom (Abrami, 1995). As an example, a class is considering several different interpersonal challenges may occur in the workplace and how they might respond. To facilitate discussion on this topic, the class is divided into groups, each with five students. Around the classroom, the faculty member has posted sheets of newsprint, creating four separate learning stations (i.e., one on each wall). At each of these stations, an interpersonal relationship scenario has also been posted for students' review, consideration, and response.

Each group has a different color. Group 1 begins at Station 1. Members of the group review the scenario at their station and provide a written response or solution on the newsprint paper. After a 5-to-10 minute period, the groups are directed to rotate in a clockwise fashion. Group 1 rotates to Station 2, Group 2 moves to Station 2, and so on. They read the scenario and previous responses and provide additional suggestions or modify previously posted comments.

After each group has been given the opportunity to review and comment on each scenario, the groups return to their home stations to reflect on the suggested responses to their assigned dilemma. They then process these suggestions and formulate a composite response to share with the entire group.

Service-Learning

The term service-learning has become a common part of conversations in higher education. Engstrom and Tinto (1997) observed although many

How Can We Meet All of Their Needs? A Class-Wide Project

Imagine that you are teaching a class that is considering the various options to resolve a pressing societal problem—reducing the prevalence of teen pregnancy. You divide the class into five groups of five members each. You then advise the class that there are several different subgroups in the community that have expressed varied perspectives on the causes of teen pregnancy and the interventions that would be most appropriate to reduce the prevalence of this problem. These groups are parents, school personnel, clergy, reproductive rights groups, and teens.

Eric, Heather, Todd, Antonio, and Shandra are assigned to work together as a group. They are designated as Team #1. Each member is then assigned (at the discretion of the group) to investigate the interests, concerns, and recommendations of one of the identified special interest groups (e.g., parents, teens). To do this, each group member will join with students from other subgroups (i.e., Team #2, #3, #4, #5) who are likewise investigating similar interests. So, for example, Eric is assigned to explore the concerns of parents. In that capacity, he meets with members of the other four class groups who also have an interest in the perspectives and opinions of parents.

After the subgroups connected with each of the specialty topics meet and discuss their area of interest, team members then return to their home group (i.e., Team #1, #2, #3, #4, #5) and share the information they have gained. The group then discusses the problem from these varied perspectives and construct their own course of action through the process of consensus building. The jigsaw comes together as the pieces of information are shared, analyzed, and assembled.

Figure 5.2. Example of a jigsaw exercise. Reprinted from *A Brief Guide for Teaching Millennial Learners* by J. B. Garner, 2007, p. 48. Copyright 2007 by Triangle Publishing. Used with permission.

institutions of higher education want students to become socially responsible, global citizens, or world changers, few actually have a conscious curricular plan for accomplishing those lofty outcomes. They propose service-learning may be one path to consider in helping students gain the insights to actually become socially responsible advocates in a global context. Rhoads (1997) defines service-learning as an integrated and reciprocal experience where service experiences are clearly linked to classroom learning:

> the students' community service experiences are compatible and integrated with the academic learning objectives of the course, in a manner similar to traditional course requirements. Here students' observations and experiences in the community setting are as pivotal to the students' academic learning as class lectures and library research. In this integrated model, the service and the learning are reciprocally related; the service experiences inform and transform the academic learning, and the academic learning informs and transforms the service experience. (p. 21)

Rhoads and Howard (1998) also call service-learning "a pedagogy of action and reflection" (p. 39). Students are called to actively engage themselves in learning and then engage in a reflective analysis of their experiences, feelings, and learning.

Weigert (1998) identified six common themes that should be considered as criteria for a true service-learning experience:

1. Students provide a meaningful service.
2. The service students provide meets an identified need or goal.
3. Members of the community are actively involved in defining the need.
4. The services provided have a direct connection to the learning outcomes of the course.
5. Students have the opportunity for reflection.
6. There is an explicit understanding that students are being evaluated on their reflections and learning—not on the fact that they have provided a service.

Edward Zlotkowski (2001), a staunch advocate and expert in the field of service-learning, articulates a natural connection between this form of pedagogy and the first-year seminar. Arguing that first-year programs, which are typically designed to acclimate students to higher education, must also prepare them for engaged citizenship in the 21st century world beyond the campus, Zlotkowski notes, "It is hard to see how first-year programs can prepare new students to maximize their learning potential unless those programs abandon the often unexamined assumption that significant academic learning takes place only on campus—in classrooms, libraries, and residence halls" (p. xiii). In effect, he has thrown down the gauntlet in relation to the importance of service-learning in facilitating the development of students who are able to look beyond themselves to a world in need and, as part of that process, envision themselves as agents of influence and change. It is important to note that he sees the first-year experience as a critical element of starting out students with that goal in mind.

As an ongoing part of the first-year seminar I teach, service-learning is a standard requirement. Students are expected to complete 10 hours of service in some location in our community over the course of the semester. Upon completion of their hours, they are required to submit a reflection paper on the experience, describing what they have done, learned, and felt as a result of the service. Additionally, they are asked to describe the ways in which this service was of benefit to the recipients. It is always interesting to note the initial expressions of dread and disinterest when students learn about this requirement. It all seems so overwhelming. And yet, at the end of the semester, when it is all said and done, students generally will point to their service-learning experience as one of the most gratifying and important undertakings of the class. This experience is intended, as part of the course content, to assist students in understanding that with minimal effort, even in the midst of a busy schedule, they can engage in service to others and make a difference in the lives of others and the world.

When thinking about service-learning in the first-year seminar, one element that adds a great deal to the experience is when faculty members serve alongside their students. This simple act communicates volumes to students. It not only says, "I think it is important you learn to serve others," but also "I am putting myself in a position of learner and servant alongside you this semester." The casual conversations that emerge from serving alongside students, and the opportunity to expand teaching beyond the walls of the classroom, are priceless and memorable.

Incorporating Service-Learning Into the First-Year Seminar

Some considerations for launching a service-learning component in the first-year seminar include

> » Analyzing course-related learning outcomes to determine possible connection points for the implementation of a service-learning requirement

» Making connections with people and agencies in the community who might have a need that corresponds to the content and focus of the course. This is the point at which the faculty member's ability to network with people on the campus and in the community becomes an important asset on behalf of students.
» Delineating expectations for student participation in the service-learning process (e.g., time commitments, behavioral expectations, documentation, formats for reflection, due dates)
» Maintaining ongoing communication with service-learning sites to monitor the quality of services being provided by students and to troubleshoot any difficulties that may arise. When serving in the community, our work and service ethic, and that of our students, sends a powerful message.
» Continually evaluating the process and the outcomes to determine better and more effective ways of integrating this experience into the pedagogy of classes.

Connecting Points

The lecture has long been a standard feature of the college classroom. Although there is a role and purpose for engaging in a lecture format, there are clear alternatives to the lecture as a primary means of teaching in the first-year seminar. These techniques, active-learning strategies, can be used in a variety of ways to promote student achievement of desired learning outcomes. The use of active-learning strategies expands the scope of possibility in providing students with opportunities to apply, connect, and contextualize course content.

The three general categories of active learning strategies discussed in this chapter include

» Cooperative learning (i.e., working in dyads or small groups to accomplish specified tasks)
» Problem-based learning (i.e., assigned tasks that engage students in critical thinking in response to a presented dilemma, scenario, or problem)
» Service-learning (i.e., service in response to an identified need along with a time of reflection)

Readers are encouraged to think about ways in which these approaches to teaching might enhance the learning experience for students in the courses they teach. In the first-year seminar, these strategies can start students on the path to becoming proficient critical thinkers.

Chapter 6
Technology as an Instructional Resource

Creative activity could be described as a type of learning process where teacher and pupil are located in the same individual.—Arthur Koestler

This chapter presents an interesting paradox. In the gap between writing and publication, it is very likely a whole variety of new instructional resources, particularly in the area of technology, have emerged and are receiving widespread use in the classroom. Descriptions of promising or potentially useful techniques and the omission of others will no doubt immediately date this book, but that is the challenge inherent in describing instructional resources in higher education. A rapid pace of innovation and development, particularly in the area of technology, has become a way of life in the 21st century. The question that remains, however, is whether higher education can stay abreast of this progress by translating new discoveries into meaningful learning tools.

The pace of technological innovation has increased rapidly since the introduction of the personal computer in the early 1980s, with technological developments becoming an integral part of our vocabulary, lives, and culture (Cordell, 2011; Lavin, Korte, & Davies, 2010; Prensky, 2001). Today, we have widespread, almost universal, access to the Internet and personal computers. PowerPoint presentations have become a ubiquitous part of the instructional landscape. Cell phones, pagers, and personal data assistants (PDAs) have evolved to smartphones, which can surf the net, manage our calendars, support document review and creation, play music and videos, take photos and videos, and place calls. We have also seen an explosion of social networking and Web 2.0 technologies (e.g., Facebook, Twitter, YouTube, blogs, wikis). New terminology (e.g., net surfing, information superhighway, website, chat room, cyber, browser, online, homepage, HTML, @) has entered the lexicon.

The advent of the current generation of college students coincides roughly with this rapid advance in technology. As a result, millennials have grown up in a culture that celebrates and covets the most current, fastest, flashiest, smallest, and most convenient forms of technology. They have also become accustomed to integrating that technology into every aspect of their lives (Pattengale & Garner, 2007). Prensky (2001) labeled this group *digital natives*, in contrast to those born before 1982, who are identified as *digital immigrants* and are always running to keep up with new technology. For the digital native, technology is simply a fact of life and something they navigate with apparent ease:

> Raised amid a barrage of information, they are able to juggle a conversation on Instant Messenger, a Web-surfing session, and an iTunes playlist while reading *Twelfth Night* for homework. Whether or not they are absorbing the fine points of the play is a matter of debate. (Scott, 2005, p. A34)

Moreover, studies produced by Chronicle Research Services (2009) and the U.S. Department of Commerce (2010) suggest students will demand increasing access to technology and to flexible learning experiences made possible by technology. For example, the U.S. Department of Commerce identifies several practices likely to increase in prevalence as students demand increasing convenience from postsecondary institutions, such as

» Students will increasingly expect access to classes from cellular phones and other portable computing devices.
» They may sign up to take a course in person, and then opt to monitor class meetings online and attend whenever they want.
» Classroom discussions, office hours with a professor, lectures, study groups, and papers will all be online. (p. 9)

For the 21st century faculty member, some number of whom will be digital immigrants, the challenge of keeping up with innovation, or staying ahead of the curve, can be a daunting task (Duderstadt, 1999). Within this chapter, we will examine two major categories of instructional resources: (a) primarily classroom-based (e.g., PowerPoint, personal response clickers, smartphones, tablet computers, electronic textbooks, podcasts, television, film) and (b) primarily Internet-based (e.g., course management systems, online course components, blogs and wikis, virtual environments, social networking).

Classroom-Based Instructional Resources

A growing variety of tools can be easily added to the repertoire of faculty teaching in the first-year seminar. The important thing to remember is selecting the appropriate collection of tools should be based upon one criterion: the level at which the chosen tools will contribute to student learning and the accomplishment of course outcomes.

PowerPoint Presentations

Perhaps the most widely used classroom-based instructional resource is the PowerPoint presentation. At the same time, this is probably the most misused classroom-based instructional resource in higher education. Goodman (2009) describes what is an all-too-common use of PowerPoint slides in the college classroom:

> On the first day of the new term, you enter the lecture theatre full of anticipation, along with 120 other students. The opening PowerPoint slide appears. Forty slides later you have planned your holiday, taken a nap or are thinking about dinner. Your enthusiasm for the subject evaporates… (p. 61)

Klemm (2007) identified four traps that can be hazardous for faculty using PowerPoint slides as a teaching tool. First, students can be eased and relaxed into a mode of coming to class, finding a comfortable location in the classroom with the expectation of being entertained much as if they were planning to watch a television program or a movie. Interestingly, Klemm proposes PowerPoint presentations filled with graphics, animations, and other features may actually increase the possibility of this occurrence. Second, PowerPoint presentations normally do not contain many provisions for direct interaction with the speaker or among the listeners. This fact may reinforce student apathy and nonparticipation. Third, and rather ironically, faculty members occasionally become so infatuated with the clever format of their own PowerPoint slides that simply showing them off to students becomes the ultimate goal.

Finally, students often become accustomed to receiving a copy of the PowerPoint slides and use this as license not to pay attention in class (or even to refrain from attending class). In fact, Gier and Kreiner (2009) investigated the effects of PowerPoint slides on learning as measured by student performance on quizzes and exams. The authors suggest that one of the common mistakes students make is the belief that studying the content of PowerPoint slides will provide all of the information they need to adequately prepare for examinations and course-related assignments. To assist students in their learning through the use of PowerPoint, the researchers strategically inserted content questions that emphasized the key learning outcomes. This process resulted in improved scores on quizzes and exams. The authors suggest that instructors strongly consider using questions and other strategies to enhance the level of active participate during the learning process.

One possible iteration of the Gier and Kreiner content-based question strategy is to advise students that a certain number of exam or quiz questions will be posed during each class contributing to their final course grade. Such an approach would obviously increase the levels at which students are attentive in class but also pinpoint the key pieces of information being communicated. Another strategy is to provide slides with fill-in-the-blank features. Students must come to class to gain the information contained in these missing parts of the PowerPoint slides.

While using PowerPoint as a teaching tool in the first-year seminar may have some drawbacks, faculty can use it successfully by considering the following recommendations:

» Use PowerPoint technology only as a way of enhancing and clarifying the content. Quite often, this technology becomes an end in itself. A PowerPoint presentation is never a substitute for insightful, well-organized content presented in an engaging manner.

» Always think of the PowerPoint presentation as an agenda rather than a script. As such, instructors must resist the strong temptation to read the entire content of the slides to the class. Rather, the instructor should assume the audience has the ability to read the materials more quickly than he or she is able to verbalize the content. Taking the time to become thoroughly familiar with the presentation will also help instructors overcome the urge to read the slides.

» Consider the periodic use of slides containing only a graphic design or picture as a prompt to tell a story or expand on a topic of concern related to the content and focus of the class.

» On a similar note, use PowerPoint slides as a jumping off point for discussion and dialogue. For example, ask the audience to respond to a picture or question, pose a provocative question on the screen, or have them discuss an issue and then share the results of a survey or research related to their discussion.

» Make sure the type is large enough to be read from the furthest point in the room.

» Similarly, make sure slides have an adequate amount of white space. Cluttered slides detract from the overall effectiveness of the presentation.

» Ensure any graphics are clear and concise. On occasion, graphics lose their clarity on the screen as they are increased in size. If a graphic is unclear on a small computer screen, that lack of clarity will be magnified when it is projected on the screen.

» Never assume students will be as dazzled and amazed by the presentation itself as much as by the content you are sharing. For example, slide animations are eye-catching and clever, but they can also eat up memory and be impacted by the power of your computer. Faculty members using animation should make sure the remote has a fully functioning battery and the computer can deliver animations at a reasonable speed that will not interfere with the pace and flow of the presentation.

» Invest in a remote control device that will allow mobility in the classroom. Interactions with students should be the centerpiece of the presentation; being tethered to the computer to change slides can impede this. For a small investment (usually around $25), faculty members will be able to move around the classroom and interact with students in a more personal manner.

Making the Most of Student Laptops

Laptop computers have become a vital component of students' educational equipment. Some will acquire a new laptop by convincing their parents it is an absolute necessity for their success in college, others will attend a college or university where students are required to purchase or lease a laptop, and, in some instances, colleges and universities will provide every incoming first-year student with a laptop computer. A study by Salaway, Caruso, and Nelson (2007) indicates a continuing trend toward personal laptop ownership (i.e., 52.8% in 2005, 68.3% in 2006, 75.8% in 2007). It is reasonable to assume this trend will continue into the future not only with laptops as we know them but also with other, as yet, unreleased forms of portable computing technology. An issue that will be of ongoing concern for colleges and universities, however, particularly in light of changing demographics, is assuring the availability of necessary computing equipment for students who are financially unable to purchase their own computers (Wilson, Wallin, & Reiser, 2003).

Faculty often express a variety of opinions on the topic of computer use in the classroom. Some embrace the presence of laptop computers, while others view them as a curse on higher education. In fact, at various times, there have been instances where faculty members have summarily banned the use of laptop computers in their classrooms (Bugeja, 2007; Chanen, 2007). The biggest complaint, of course, is that students are using laptops for purposes other than attending to the activities and discussion of the classroom (e.g., watching movies, television programs and sporting events; communicating with friends via social networks; completing assignments for other classes). The standard response from many students, but millennials in particular, is the multitask defense, which promotes the idea they are totally capable of doing many things at once. In other words, students believe they can take notes in class, talk with their friends on Facebook, and tweet their plans for the evening, while remaining on pace with the activities. The jury is still out on whether multitasking is truly possible (i.e., I can do more than one thing at a time and do them all well) or simply results in doing many things simultaneously but at a mediocre level (Borst, Taatgen, & van Rijn, 2010; Gasser & Palfrey, 2009).

Interestingly, the research on the use of laptop computers in the classroom is rather inconsistent but does not clearly point to the use of these devices as a significant boost to learning (Pascarella & Terenzini, 2005). Weaver and Nilson (2005) argue in spite of the fact that higher education did not adequately prepare for the onslaught of laptop computers, these devices are probably here to stay, and it behooves us to begin making the best of the situation through the creation of a new collection of teaching strategies. They offer a variety of ideas in this area, including

» In-class online learning style and preference assessments
» Directed searches of websites for information pertinent to classroom discussions
» Virtual first-day introductory information cards
» Immediate feedback on in-class presentations
» Writing responses to concepts and ideas presented in class
» Simulations

These strategies are only the beginning of what lies ahead in capitalizing on the power and potential of computers in the classroom. The level at which this innovation develops, however, largely depends on the response of faculty and the speed with which they embrace the technology, accept the role computers can play in the classroom, and engage in the process of integrating computer use into the instructional process (Fried, 2008).

Audience Response Systems

A strategy for enhancing PowerPoint presentations and inviting student participation is the use of audience response systems. These response systems often take the form of a small handheld device that allows students to register responses to questions posed on a PowerPoint slide.[1] Students are then given a specified period of time to log their opinion or response. When the time expires, the faculty member activates a slide-based mechanism that displays the results for the class (i.e., percentages and graphs summarizing the group's responses). As an important feature of this process, faculty must develop skills in quickly analyzing the presented results and crafting questions inviting further analysis and group interaction.

Masikunis, Panayiotidis, and Burke (2009) examined the perception and impact of using audience response systems in the college classroom. Their observations indicate the significance of effective planning in the selection of circumstances where the clickers are employed. This would imply using a response system as simply a way to make the class more interesting may lead to a negative response from students. Audience response systems, therefore, should always be viewed as a tool for advancing learning goals. The strategies Masikunis et al. recommend include the use of digital video clips depicting relevant scenarios requiring a solution, case studies inviting perceptual choices (e.g., What will happen next?), and slides including links to websites with follow-up questions related to their content. Finally, it is proposed audience response systems, in addition to their role in promoting individual student response and participation options, can serve as an impetus to creating small-group discussions (Moss & Crowley, 2011).

One of the inherent benefits of personal response systems is the way in which even the most reticent students can express their opinions and participate in the flow of a class. As questions are posed, students who normally may sit on the sidelines while more confident and verbal students express their opinions, now have a mechanism to engage in the conversation even if they are not comfortable sharing their opinions verbally.

---

[1] At the time of this writing, many publishers bundled personal response clickers along with their textbooks. Additionally, vendors commonly sold software that linked personal response technology with smartphones, tablets, and laptop computers. Under this scenario, students only needed to download the necessary software to their phone or laptop computer in preparation for participating in personal response activities. There was sometimes a cost associated with registration of this software.

Tablet Computers and Smartphones

The melodies and alarms emanating from cellular telephones have become a familiar part of our daily auditory experience. As we participate in various types of group meetings and conversations, we typically have little response when a member of the group is alerted to a call, e-mail, or text message. Despite a growing acceptance of the need to be digitally available at all times, college faculty often respond with a sense of indignation when a lecture or class activity is interrupted by these all-too-familiar sounds. Many faculty devise stringent rules and deliver eloquent monologues on the consequences of cell phone usage in the classroom. This indignation sometimes flies in the face of administrative policies on cell phone availability as a counter measure and communication tool in the instance of campus emergencies (Kennedy, 2009).

Caverly, Ward, and Caverly (2009) make strong arguments encouraging higher education faculty to redefine the role and purpose of cell phones to include opportunities for participation in the instructional process. First, they argue, while all students may not have access to laptop computers (i.e., described above as a potential challenge for lower SES students), virtually all students have access to cell phones. Additionally, as this technology continues to develop and become more accessible, cell phones will inevitably have many of the same search and interactive capabilities we currently attribute to laptop computers. Brown (2010) coined the term *mobile learning* to describe this new direction for capitalizing on a piece of technology that can be found in the pocket or backpack of virtually every student: "Mobile learning is the exploitation of ubiquitous handheld technologies, together with wireless and mobile phone networks to facilitate, support, and enhance and extend the reach of teaching and learning" (p. 28).

Here are some ways in which faculty can consider using cell phones as a teaching resource in the first-year seminar:

» Kinsella (2009) suggests the possibility of inviting students to text questions and comments to faculty members as a way of enhancing feedback and responding to students' questions and concerns.
» The website www.polleverywhere.com provides a free service allowing (up to 30) students to respond to polling questions using their cellular phones.
» With the emergence of applications or apps for smartphones (e.g., iPhone, Android, BlackBerry), it is entirely possible faculty could develop course-specific applications providing students with additional learning

opportunities and resources. Pursell (2009), for example, proposed smartphones could hold flash cards and other learning aids to assist students in acquiring needed information in courses, such as organic chemistry.

» With increasing movements toward asynchronous learning as an option in higher education, the smartphone could be a viable platform for promoting online discussion groups.

Electronic Textbooks

There is a growing buzz about the level at which electronic textbooks will inevitably change the face of higher education. This phenomenon has been fueled by the emergence of commercial products, such as the Kindle and Apple's iPad. These products make it easy and relatively inexpensive to download entire books in a matter of seconds. Barack (2006) suggests that as computers become smaller, more powerful, less expensive, and stocked with unique software applications, electronic textbooks become more likely.

Kingsbury and Galloway (2006) have predicted that publishers, in order to gain a competitive edge in this potentially profitable market, will need to move beyond simply digitizing textbooks so they can be read on a computer screen. Rather, they will need to think creatively about the variety of bells and whistles that can be used to distinguish their products from all the others in a highly competitive and crowded market (e.g., video clips, audio enhancements, links to websites, embedded quizzes and assessments). So, for example, as students are reading about an event in history, they will have the opportunity to link from their textbook to a video clip or a website. The other advantage of this approach is these supplemental resources (as well as the content of the textbook) can be updated and revised as new events and discoveries occur (Thomas & Brown, 2011).

A key variable in the evolution of textbook technology will ultimately hinge on the responses of faculty and students. While it might be reasonable to assume millennials will be attracted to electronic textbooks, surveys by Sheppard, Grace, and Koch (2008) reveal students may have some misgivings about electronic textbooks and their ability to make this transition. In all likelihood, this probably has more to do with a lack of familiarity rather than an outright rejection of electronic texts as a learning resource. Further, as electronic books begin to demonstrate sales growth in the popular or bestseller market, it is reasonable to speculate student attitudes toward this media format will change and achieve increased popularity (Deahl, 2010).

Podcasts

Lum (2006) notes, "more than 80 percent of college students own at least one device that can download and play recordings" (p. 33). The ubiquity of such devices suggests podcasts, audio or video files, or documents broadcast over the Internet and available to download and replay at the convenience of the user, may be a natural way to provide students with learning resources that either reinforce or extend what happens in the classroom. Hew (2009) identifies some of the instructional benefits inherent in podcasting. First, he proposes, listening is an instinctual activity (as opposed to reading) and, therefore, is often compatible with the ways in which students learn. Second, and probably most important to students, podcasts are remarkably convenient and a natural match for the nocturnal lifestyles of college students. Finally, the convenience and availability of the Internet provides a wonderful resource for storage and accessibility. Students and faculty, therefore, will not be encumbered with tapes, discs, and other storage paraphernalia.

Faculty, however, are quick to note the availability of podcasts could serve as a disincentive to actually attend class since they can be downloaded and listened to in a dorm room (Read, 2005; Young 2010). To counteract this concern, faculty might create attendance policies requiring students to attend class and only make the podcasts available as a means of reviewing and reinforcing what was covered in class. Podcasts might also be used to provide enrichment materials students can watch or listen to as an out-of-class assignment (Panday, 2007).

Students could also be required to create podcasts as a course assignment (Panday, 2007). This approach forces students to use an emerging technology while also requiring them to engage with course content. In such a model, students might be charged with the responsibility of creating podcasts connected to topics that will be discussed in class. Alternately, student-produced podcasts might expand the reach of the course by exploring interesting and relevant topics not part of the established course content.

Television and Film

The culture of our planet, to a large extent, is becoming accustomed to and perhaps dependent upon, receiving large amounts of information in visual formats (e.g., Internet pages, podcasts, television, movies). Although there is often a tendency to regard visual media as fluffy and vapid, this venue holds great pedagogical potential. Discussions that connect students with television and film provide an excellent way of contextualizing course content (Basham & Nardone, 1997; Bluestone, 2000; Liles, 2007). This technique is particularly applicable in the first-year seminar. For example, showing a clip from a popular film or television show can promote critical thinking as students consider the impact of the plot, the personalities and values of the characters, the overall narrative, and the choices characters make as well as the resulting consequences of those choices. Assignments and discussions can encourage students to analyze these circumstances and make applications to their own lives and challenges.

On my own campus, as part of the first-year seminar, students participate in the GlobeFest Film Festival, which exposes them to the experience of watching movies in a community, engaging in a critical analysis of the stories being told, and assessing their relevance to current events and crises in our world. This process has become an excellent means of including the input and expertise of faculty from a variety of disciplines (e.g., psychology, social work, history, economics, literature) who serve a respondents and discussion facilitators.

Web-Based Instructional Resources

There is little doubt the Internet has dramatically altered our world (e.g., access to global communication, the pace of communication, immediate access to vast amounts of information). We have become insatiable consumers of information and incessant digital communicators. To be anywhere, at any time, without immediate access to the World Wide Web is perceived as a major inconvenience. Although higher education has made tremendous strides in taking advantage of this resource as a teaching tool, much remains to be done. As might be expected, individual faculty members have varied levels of comfort and expertise in using technology for their own purposes. Some faculty members have difficulty determining the ways in which technology can be effectively integrated into the flow of their courses. For the purposes of our discussion here, we will review some of the tools commonly finding their way into college classes.

Course Management Systems

Course Management Systems (CMS) are software that create course websites and provide a variety of resources for faculty and students (e.g., electronic versions of course syllabi and other resources, links to articles and videos, online assessment tools, discussion forums, class topics and schedules, grades, tools for detecting plagiarism). Examples of commonly used CMS include Blackboard, WebCT, and Moodle. Korchmaros and Gump (2009) note that using CMS "take[s] advantage of today's college students' technological skills and usage preferences to provide course-related information and to encourage involvement in courses" (p. 161). They also point out that certain features of these systems (e.g., discussion groups, bulletin boards) allow students to "use CMS to communicate with classmates and instructors, much the same as they use social networking sites" (p. 161).

As with other instructional resources, one of the key determinants of success centers around the comfort level of faculty and students in both using the CMS technology and accessing support services when problems arise. Faculty teaching in first-year seminars may wish to consider helping students orient themselves to the vast number of resources common to a CMS. This orientation will not only assist them in achieving success in the first-year seminar but also help them in accessing similar information for other courses on their academic schedules.

Online Course Components

As has been described, one of the waves of the future will be the expectation that courses are offered in more convenient formats and times (Chronicle Research Services, 2009). Online courses, whether taught exclusively in that manner or as part of a blended model including live components, will undoubtedly continue to increase in number and variety. Lewis and Abdul-Hamid (2006) have observed that although there has been ongoing concern about the lack of rigor and pedagogy in online courses, some promising strategies and related research are emerging in this area of instruction. For example, Shank (2007) suggests a plethora of ways in which online learning can be an enriching and invigorating experience. These include collaborative efforts (e.g., group projects, collaborative writing), discussion groups (e.g., synchronous and asynchronous, evaluations of the quality and contributory nature of participating in discussions), self-directed asynchronous activities (e.g., creating and completing tables or charts, entering answers to questions and then comparing those responses with the opinions of experts, timed evaluation tasks, sharing of bookmarks and web resources), synchronous activities (e.g., moderating discussions, flash cards and reviews, creation of concept maps and webs), and self-check activities and assessments (e.g., interactive games, quizzes and tests that can be repeated numerous times to promote mastery of content). Creating these options will require that faculty have a willingness to think in new ways and the time necessary to master these approaches to learning.

Reflecting on the application of online course components to the first-year seminar, faculty may choose to consider a hybrid option that includes face-to-face classroom time, discussions, and activities along with an online component. This would allow students to gain learning experiences in both types of instructional arrangements. Graham (2006) describes *blended learning* to include possibilities for combinations of instructional methodologies, methods, and online and face-to-face instruction. Jung and Suzuki (2006) provide several examples of how blended learning opportunities can include open interaction (e.g., small group debates and discussion), knowledge creation (e.g., interactions with experts, synchronous and asynchronous exchanges of ideas), distribution of information (e.g., posting articles, tracking students' viewing of posted information), and efficient management (e.g., electronic submission of assignments, opportunities for posting feedback).

Blogs

Tim Berners-Lee, the engineer and computer scientist credited with the creation of the World Wide Web, actually had a vision for the web as a place where people would not only be able read but also write (Richardson, 2006). Two of the more popular approaches to writing on the web are *blogs* and *wikis*. A blog (short for weblog) is a website allowing contributors to share their thoughts and feelings on one or more topics, questions, or issues. Comments are posted in reverse chronological order (i.e., the most recent entry is listed first) and can be read by anyone who has access and logs on to the site. The writing on blogs can range from lengthy essays to quick, brief responses to the work of others. Quite often, bloggers will use specialized and commonly known abbreviations to express their ideas. As of 2009, there were more than 126 million blogs (Pingdom, 2010).

Students often spend great amounts of time reading and responding to the information found on blog sites. Likewise, many faculty members sponsor their own blogs as a means of expressing their thoughts and opinions on a variety of topics. In one class offered in 2010, my students were asked to select and read an article on an Internet website related to the topic of the course. They were then asked to log on to a blog site designed specifically for the course and record a response to the article they had read. The responses were far deeper than I had expected or observed on previous assignments. I have a working hypothesis that, on some level, the blog is one of the most comfortable writing venues for millennial students—compatible with their dominant forms of communication.

Wikis

A wiki is an accessible website providing the opportunity for readers to contribute new information and collaboratively edit existing content. In the realm of wikis, Wikipedia, a free online encyclopedia, has the distinction of being singled out by faculty as the website that cannot be used in the creation of research papers. This pronouncement is made due to the general perception that information shared on open-content sites simply cannot be trusted because there is no oversight in regard to accuracy. Yet, the power of this collaborative tool is chronicled by Richardson (2006) in relation to the Indian Ocean earthquake of 2004:

> The event occurred just after midnight (GMT) on December 26, and the first 76-word post was created at Wikipedia about 9 hours later. Twenty-four hours after the first mention, the entry had been edited more than 400 times and had grown to about 3,000 words, complete with some of the first photographs of the devastation, a chart documenting the dead and injured, and other graphics describing how the tsunami was spawned. . . . It was without question the most comprehensive resource on the Web about that horrific event. (p. 61)

What may concern faculty is that such descriptions, although timely, do not provide opportunities for verification of the vast number of entries or accuracy of the facts posted.

However, wikis need not be rejected out of hand; rather, they could be used as an important exercise in critical thinking. For virtually anything we read, whether on Wikipedia, another website, a journal article, or a book, there is a need to be vigilant about the content and its veracity. This may be a great place to start with first-year students. As an assignment, for example, students could pick a topic of interest and examine the entries that have been made on Wikipedia and the sources cited as verification. Students could be asked to review this information, check out the sources, and provide a written critique of the entry. Additionally, they could be required to provide their own sources of information that either affirm or debunk the Wikipedia citations.

Another option is to have students create their own wikis. The sponsors of Wikipedia provide specific directions for creating an article on a new topic. Students could be asked to generate a series of topics related to course content and worthy of their investigation. At the end of the semester, they could be evaluated on the quality and organization of their wiki. As an alternative, teams might develop articles and serve as constructive critics for other groups. This interactive dialogue should increase student involvement and, ultimately, the quality of their work.

Virtual Learning Environments

The term *virtual learning environment* (VLE) is used in a variety of ways within the professional literature of higher education. McGill and Hobbs (2008), describes a VLE as "an information system that facilitates e-learning. VLEs process, store, and disseminate educational material and support communication associated with teaching and learning" (p. 191). This definition could include, for example, something as simple as a course management system and as complex as "virtual environments like *Second Life* . . . where residents create avatars (three-dimensional [3-D] self-representations) and navigate around an online virtual environment in which students engage in interactions through the means of an avatar" (Burgess & Caverly, 2009, p. 42).

This form of technology will continue to evolve and develop (Dittmer, 2010). As the growth process transpires, it is also very likely faculty will create new and interesting uses for this technology. These developments will lead to circumstances where faculty can create lifelike simulations in a variety of contexts using 3D-VLEs. As an example, instead of creating an online experience centering on a collection of documents, video clips, and podcasts, 3D-VLEs will provide students with the opportunity to engage in real-time interactions and completely immerse themselves in presented scenarios. The lifelike nature of this technology adds a new level of personal engagement in the learning process.

Social Networking

Social networking is undoubtedly the most significant technological phenomenon of the early 21st century. The level at which people of all ages and walks of life are connected through website like Facebook and Twitter is astounding. According to the Facebook website, as of 2011, there are more than 750 million registered users, 50% of them log on to the website daily, and the average member has 130 friends. At the same time, Twitter reported 400 million users (Heath, 2011). The basic process involves registering for the service, creating a website with personal information, inviting people to become friends or followers, and then engaging in ongoing conversations and updates about life events.

The dynamics of social networking are fascinating. This electronic venue provides participants with the opportunity to connect with people who are part of their distant past, share pictures and written accounts of the events in their lives, and keep up with the lives of friends and relatives in a highly efficient manner. For college students, these locations have become an important way of socializing and connecting. In 2009, I spent a semester abroad with a group of college students in Zambia. Internet services were often interrupted and difficult to maintain. When the services were available, however, the first place students went to get updates and share pictures of their adventures was Facebook (as opposed to university-related sites where they were expected to complete online assignments). In a matter of minutes, they were able to converse with friends, share the latest news of their Zambian experience, and find out what was going on in the lives of their friends. With the instant messaging feature of Facebook, they were often able to communicate in real time.

For faculty, social networking media often create a series of dilemmas. The first centers on whether to engage current students as friends, thereby allowing them access to varying of amounts of personal information (e.g., pictures, family information, conversations with other friends). The line between being a friend and a faculty member with some measure of authority over the student is often difficult to discern. There is reason to believe students have a positive view of faculty who are transparent and demonstrate their care for students by sharing information about who they are as people (e.g., interests, passions, academic experiences, community and service experiences). The challenge, however, is where that line should be drawn and to what extent information divulged on Facebook violates that imaginary and somewhat arbitrary line. Thus, Mazer, Murphy, and Simonds (2009) acknowledge the potential benefit of using "Facebook as a way to foster their relationship with students" but also encourage faculty to "proceed with caution" (p. 181).

After making a decision about whether to enroll on a social network and who to include as friends, faculty may wonder how to employ social networks as pedagogical tools. Selwyn (2009) coined the term *Faceworking* to capture the use of this technology as a learning tool in higher education. Examples of Faceworking include written reflections, dialogues on assigned readings, and responding to one another's work. So, for example, students might be required to post a written reflection on a portion of course content and additionally provide a response (e.g., affirmation, critique, clarification) to the work of a classmate. This strategy has been employed in the first-year seminar I teach. Anecdotally, students appear to engage in deeper levels of thinking and writing when they know their work will be available for review by their peers.

Young (2010) explored the implications of using Twitter as a classroom-teaching tool. He warns his particular strategy is not for the faint of heart, as the Tweets (i.e., 140-character text messages) offered by students can be challenging, critical, and caustic. Yet, he describes a college professor who teaches in a large auditorium setting and who provides an opportunity for students to Tweet questions, comments, and observations during class. This practice gives students an opportunity to engage with the instructor while providing the instructor with immediate feedback or questions from students. This engagement can take classroom learning in unexpectedly positive or negative directions. As such, the use of interactive media in the classroom is likely to be most successful when it is grounded in the context of a solid relationship between the faculty member and students.

A final consideration that has particular relevance for the first-year seminar is the process of reminding students of the differences between writing comments on a social network page, or in an e-mail or text message, and writing in the context of college assignments (e.g., research papers, written reflections, written responses to examination questions). Far too frequently, first-year students will relapse into using text language (e.g., LOL for *laugh out loud*, 10Q for *thank you*, CUL for *see you later*) or inappropriately informal greetings (e.g., Hey Dude!). First-year faculty will do their students a great service by addressing the appropriate uses of language and greetings in varied contexts.

Connecting Points

As has been described, the World Wide Web is a vast territory with unbelievable amounts of information. Although it is presumably common knowledge not all of the information on the web is good (i.e., reliable, factual, or accurate), there is often a tendency to accept what has been written as the truth, as evidenced by the justification "I saw it on the Internet". To be fair, we must also acknowledge that careful and judicious use of the Internet can be a tremendous boon to our ability to perform required tasks and gain information in a remarkably efficient manner. One skill we can teach our students that will serve them during their college years and well beyond is the process of discerning truth from fiction on the Internet.

Relatively speaking, we are only at the early stages of exploring the ways in which technology can impact and enhance teaching and learning. It is safe to assume technology will always be part of the higher education landscape. The challenge for faculty remains one of balancing several key elements: (a) remaining abreast of current technologies, (b) assessing the degree to which emerging technologies can be applied in the classroom, and (c) creating ways to integrate technology into the classroom (or outside the classroom) in a manner that enhances the learning experience for all participating students.

Chapter 7
Assessment of Student Learning

Everything that can be counted does not necessarily count; everything that counts cannot necessarily be counted. —Albert Einstein

We are living in a time of accountability and assessment. A growing number of books, professional journal articles, accreditation visits, conferences, and webinars have assessment embedded in the content. Faculty members are being asked to demonstrate greater attention to the manner in which they measure and document student achievement in relation to course and program learning outcomes. In this climate, it is critically important for faculty to have a clear response to the question, What are your students learning and how do you know? In the vast majority of American classrooms, one of the primary means of assessing student learning will come under the guise of tests, quizzes, and examinations. For many of the more than 18 million students enrolled in degree-granting institutions during the 2009-2010 academic year, it is very likely written examinations were a significant determining factor in assessing the degree to which they learned the required course content (often interpreted as their final grades). Extrapolating from the work of Milton (1986), if each of these students enrolled in an average of eight courses per year, and each course involved an average of two tests, there were more than 288 million objective tests (complete with bubble sheets) given during the 2009-2010 academic year. However, it is unclear what such testing tells us about student learning.

This chapter focuses on the assessment of student learning, exploring the topic from two perspectives: (a) the performances or activities in which students engage to demonstrate learning and (b) the methods instructors use to evaluate those performances or measure student learning. Before examining those strategies, we define two different philosophical approaches to assessment.

Traditional Versus Alternative Assessment

Most of the discussion regarding classroom assessment and student learning has focused on the inherent differences between the somewhat loosely defined categories of *traditional* and *alternative* assessments. Traditional assessment measures are typically written tests composed of objective questions in varying formats, including true/false, multiple-choice, fill-in-the-blank, and matching (Montgomery, 2002). Alternative assessments provide students with a format for creating a response to prompts or questions. These responses can be written, verbal, or in the form of a product (e.g., portfolio, poster, digital production) or performance (e.g., presentation, demonstration). Davies and Wavering (1999) note that alternative assessments are frequently authentic, meaning "the assessment mirrors applications of the assessed ability in real-life nonacademic settings" and they "focus on process as well as product" (p. 39).

Traditional assessments have been criticized for a variety of reasons. First, a key principle of traditional assessments is the verifiability of a correct answer for every question. As such, they reinforce a view of student learning as mastering isolated pieces of information. Further, such a view assumes the overall effectiveness of teaching and learning can be reduced to the level at which students recall such information on quizzes and tests. Second, traditional assessments provide limited opportunities for students to employ critical thinking skills in relation to course content. Third, it is arguably illogical to think the information and concepts contained in 12 hours of lectures and 200 pages of reading can be reasonably condensed into 50 multiple-choice questions. Given these concerns, can it be assumed high test scores on traditional assessments are indicative of good learning? (Anderson, 1998; Cahn, 1994; Cameron, 1991; McDaniel, 1994; Murray, 1990; Sanders, 2001). Sanders for example, suggests there may be a role of objective testing as a way of determining the level at which students are acquiring basic, discipline-specific information. This is often accomplished through the use of objective measures. However, college-level learning outcomes frequently focus on analysis, synthesis, and evaluation—skills that cannot be measured via objective tests.

Supporters of the traditional mode of assessment generally focus their efforts on the process of creating the good test and emphasize the importance of reliability and validity in the mechanics of question construction. For example, Haladyna, Downing, and Rodriguez (2002) focused on the validation of 31 guidelines for writing multiple-choice items they believe should be given serious consideration in the construction of classroom assessments.

Examples include avoiding opinion-based items, using *all of the above* as a response option, maintaining consistency in grammatical structure across response options, and varying the location of the correct answers (e.g., a, b, c, d). Good test proponents take very seriously the methodological aspects of assessment and the obligation of test developers to adhere to these conventions as opposed to the question of whether traditional assessments have a role in the university classroom.

According to Davies and Wavering (1999), "alternative assessments include a variety of techniques and strategies, such as: performance, portfolio, cooperative learning groups, peer teaching, exit cards, exhibitions, demonstrations of understanding, simulations, [and] observations, among others" (p. 39). The promotion of such strategies is often approached from two perspectives: (a) a frontal attack on the perceived inadequacies of traditional assessments with a corresponding promotion of alternative assessment strategies (Anderson, 1998) or (b) the attachment of alternative assessment strategies to commonly valued theories of teaching and learning including constructivism, Bloom's Taxonomy, multiple intelligences, and brain-based learning (Bostock, 1998; Davies & Wavering, 1999; Diaz-Lefebvre, 2004; McDaniel, 1994; Montgomery, 2002; Sanders 2001).

A Standard of Judicious Use

Although proponents of traditional and alternative assessments may continue to advocate the use of a particular approach to assessment while discounting others, the reality is that there is a logical role in higher education for both traditional and alternative assessments. Rather than spending energy in the defense of a position, educators would be well advised to generate and refine a decision-making model that would assist faculty in determining the assessment technique most appropriate for the content, skills, and applications being taught. In other words, we need to identify standards for judicious use of traditional assessment strategies. The following considerations, for example, provide a starting place for making decisions about assessment:

» Classroom assessments should be teacher-directed, mutually beneficial (i.e., students in learning, faculty in the assessment of teaching), formative, context-specific (i.e., responsive to the needs and characteristics of students, teachers, and disciplines), ongoing, and rooted in good teaching practice (Angelo & Cross, 1993).

» Good practice in assessment results in (a) improved teaching and learning, (b) a focus on what is maximally relevant, and (c) a mechanism for informing students about what they know or can do (Wergin, 1988).

» Effective assessment is contingent on the instructor's ability to define measurable outcomes, concentrate on higher level thinking and problem solving, and create criterion-referenced standards that promote mastery (McDaniel, 1994).

» Assessment tasks should be visible and meaningful pieces of work capable of standing on their own (Barr, 2003).

The selection of assessment strategies should focus on whether they accomplish specific goals rather than on the means of assessment (i.e., traditional vs. alternative assessment). More important, assessment strategies should be intentional and designed to promote student learning.

Emerging Strategies for Assessment in the First-Year Seminar

There are a number of techniques that can be used to assess student learning in the first-year seminar. The exact combination of assessment techniques instructors choose will depend largely on the learning outcomes of the seminar and the types of knowledge, skills, and dispositions that are the focus of the class. To assist in considering the options, we first examine two ways to structure opportunities for students to demonstrate learning: (a) variations on traditional objective testing procedures and (b) authentic learning experiences. The final section of the chapter will examine strategies for measuring student performance in authentic learning activities.

Variations on Traditional Objective Testing Procedures

Despite the criticisms that can be legitimately lodged against the exclusive use of objective testing procedures, it is sometimes appropriate to employ these strategies as a means of determining acquisition of basic knowledge and information. Some innovations on traditional assessment are described below.

The No-Fault Quiz. As reported by Sporer (2001), students often ask the question, Can I get extra credit? One way to provide this opportunity in a meaningful way is the No-Fault Quiz. Students are given a 5- to 15-question quiz (i.e., multiple-choice, true/false, fill-in-the-blank) covering the previous week's content. Points gained on the No-Fault Quiz count as extra credit, while points missed do not count against the student. Answers to the questions are provided immediately after the quiz. Student performance is recorded, and students take away the quiz questions, which can later serve as a source for review.

Online quizzes. Many of the current learning management systems (e.g., CNet, Blackboard) provide a mechanism for online quizzes. Quiz questions can be true/false, multiple-choice, or fill-in-the-blank. Moreover, quizzes can be open and available for student use during a specified window of time, structured to provide immediate feedback on performance, and designed for students to complete multiple times as a means of promoting content mastery. Additionally, these systems typically load the student's scores directly into the grade book for the course.

We have been using online quizzes in our first-year seminar as a means of holding students accountable for instructional content from classroom learning experiences and assigned readings. Students are responsible for completing a weekly quiz covering the presented materials and content. They can actually take the quiz up to three times during the week (with only their last score counting toward their grade). Although students often complain about the rigor imposed by this plan, there have been dramatic increases in midterm and final examination grades. We attribute these increases to the fact that students must maintain the pace of reviewing class materials and assigned readings as a way of bolstering their performance on the weekly quizzes.

The question bank. To promote learning and emphasize the most critical aspects of course content, students are provided with a bank of potential test questions (for which they must find the answers). Quite often, test publishers will provide a bank of test questions to accompany course texts. Students can then read along in the text and find the answers to the presented questions. Actual test items are selected from this bank of questions.

Learning partners. A study by Bloom (2009) revealed the benefits of collaborative testing in higher education. After a solo attempt on an examination, students were given a second attempt in a collaborative group using textbooks and class notes. Not surprisingly, their performance on the second administration of the examination was significantly improved. Students' long-term retention of course content also showed significant improvement.

To implement collaborative testing, students are assigned a learning partner as they arrive for class. During the testing period, students will work cooperatively with their partners to complete the exam. While students will complete their own answer sheets, they will also be free to discuss their opinions on the correct answers with their partners. After the examination is complete, students retain their answer sheets as the faculty member reviews and discusses the correct responses (Parkyn, 1999; Pray & Tracy, 1999; Russo & Warren, 1999; Stearns, 1996).

50/50. At the conclusion of a unit of study, students complete an online examination that includes objective questions on the current topic of discussion. The second component of the assessment process is completed in the classroom in small groups of two or three students. For this component, students are permitted to use their textbooks and class notes to cooperatively complete a series of questions requiring application, evaluation, and synthesis of course content. Each portion of the assessment (i.e., objective online assessment, classroom-based cooperative learning activity) counts as 50% of the student's assigned grade.

Following Up on Assessments

There is a tendency to administer a classroom test and then simply provide students with their individual results in the form of a percentage, a letter grade, or the number of correct responses. This practice conveys a message that the score or result is of higher importance than the learning that occurred. If learning continues during the process of classroom assessment, students should be provided with an opportunity to compare their responses with those considered to be correct.

One way to extend learning beyond test administration is to allot classroom time for a review of the test and the correct answers. Quite often, this conversation will lead to student-driven questions about the correct answers provided by faulty. This type of discussion is healthy and productive and occasionally results in a conclusion that multiple correct answers may exist for a question. The process sharpens students' ability to express and logically support their positions.

Authentic Learning Experiences

Ultimately, as our students graduate, they will find themselves in situations calling for the application of the knowledge, skills, and dispositions acquired during their college experience. They will be entering that place often referred to as the real world. Chun (2010) suggests one way faculty can better prepare students for their transition to reality beyond the classroom is through the thoughtful use of authentic assessments. These assessment tasks place the students into a scenario where they must make the best possible decisions with the information they have at their disposal. This process often leads students to discover a perfect decision is not possible, and they must choose between two mediocre options. Such is life in the real world. Strategies for engaging students in authentic learning experiences are described below.

Problem solvers. Like learning partners, the problem-solver approach allows students to collaborate to complete an evaluation activity. For example, students enrolled in Introduction to Nursing Practice are given a take-home examination that requires the development of written responses to a series of scenarios. To complete this exercise, students are assigned to a small group for the purpose of discussing the scenarios and developing the required written response. Each team grapples with the presented problem and jointly develops a response. After each group completes the written response, interactive strategies (e.g., critiques and comments, discussion in small groups) are facilitated by faculty to assist the students in processing their written products. Teams are then reconvened and given the option of refining and expanding their original work.

Discussion boards. Many online learning management systems provide a mechanism for the creation of discussion groups. Faculty members can post discussion prompts and also serve as participants in class discussions. Students are asked to make a specified number of responses to the presented prompts. These responses can be original thoughts related to the prompt or play off the comments of others (e.g., a reaction, agreement, disagreement to the comments of others).

In circumstances where an online learning system does not provide the discussion board option, faculty can use one of the many free blog sites available on the web. These sites typically require faculty and students register for the service. At the same time, however, the discussions can be restricted to identified members of the class and prohibit participation from individuals who are not enrolled.

The Letter Home. The first semester in college probably marks one of the most significant times of change in the lives of our students. One way of helping students summarize and synthesize these experiences is The Letter Home assignment. In the first-year seminar, students are asked to write a letter to someone important to them (e.g., parent, brother, sister, high school teacher, youth pastor, guidance counselor, coach) summarizing the lessons they are learning during their first semester in college. Students can even be encouraged to actually send the letter to their identified recipient. As another means for processing this information, students are provided with an opportunity to share selected content from their letters in a small-group format during class. Students are always amazed about the level at which they share common experiences and challenges with their classmates.

Classroom presentations. As we think about the fact that our students are planning for careers in a variety of fields, a skill that is always transferrable and valuable is the ability to make presentations before a group. Presentations can take a variety of forms: communicating information, teaching a skill, or persuading the audience to make a decision or take action on topics of concern. Backes and Brown (2009) offer suggestions for incorporating student presentations into instructional time:

» Provide clear directions and make sure students understand the expectations.

» Set clear time limits for the presentation.

» Require an outline and give feedback on the outline prior to the presentation.

» Require interaction with the audience, which helps students learn to think on their feet and use their problem-solving skills.

» Use a rubric or rating sheet for assessing the presentation (p. 35)

The ability to make quality presentations before a group is a skill students can use throughout their entire lives. Requiring this experience during the first-year seminar can be a good icebreaker for students in regard to making presentations in a college classroom. It is also an excellent location to provide some basic instruction on planning, using technology, interacting with the audience, and incorporating effective openers and closers.

Strategies for Assessing Authentic Learning Experiences

Since authentic performances do not lend themselves to Scantron grading, instructors need to employ different types of evaluation methods. This section describes rubrics, portfolios, and evaluation menus, which are three strategies faculty can use to assess students engaged in authentic learning experiences.

Evaluation Menu

As teachers, we all strive to provide instructional opportunities maximizing the degree to which our students gain new information, understanding, skills, and concepts. Quite often, however, course syllabi reveal a one-size-fits-all mentality. Although we know that each of our students learns differently and brings varied levels of competence and skill to the classroom, everyone is required to do identical assignments and tasks over the course of a semester. An à la carte approach to assessment choices acknowledges individual differences, demonstrates learning can occur in a variety of ways, and provides students with an opportunity to select their own learning activities. This can be implemented in three easy steps:

1. Identifying the basic learning activities and course requirements all students should complete. Examples might include reading assigned text(s); attending class; engaging in class discussions; or participating in tests, quizzes, and examinations.
2. Creating a menu of additional activities students can choose from as a way of demonstrating their learning and applying that learning in a new context. Figure 7.1 offers a sample menu.
3. Assigning point values to the various required and optional experiences comprising the assessment system

Rubrics

Rubrics are evaluation instruments that provide a set of standards and expectations related to particular assignments or overall course learning outcomes. In their simplest form, rubrics provide parameters for students as they complete assigned tasks (e.g., the specific components and expectations of the assessment process) and faculty members as they evaluate the final product. For example, if a student is required to give a classroom presentation, the performance might be assessed in relation to eight specific competencies: the chosen topic, communication of the presentation's purpose, language use, vocal variety, articulation, nonverbal behaviors, the use of media, and the appropriateness of their attire (Dunbar, Brooks, & Kubicka-Miller, 2006). By reviewing the available rubric, students will know, for example, that appropriate attire will be assessed on a 4-point scale, with 1 being the best score: business attire, very professional look = 1; casual business attire = 2; casual business attire, but seemed somewhat wrinkled = 3; and attire generally not appropriate for audience (i.e., jeans, t-shirt, shorts) = 4. These types of definitions would be available for each of the evaluative categories.

The following is a list of potential items that could be included in a learning menu (along with some ideas regarding point values based upon a 1,000 point scale). Each of these items has been tested in the field. Readers will need to judge the relevance of these activities to their own discipline or the degree to which they should be modified.

Interviews of Professionals in the Field (200 points)
Interview a minimum of three professionals currently employed in the human services field (e.g., teacher, social worker, psychologist, probation officer). Prepare a summary of your interviews, synthesizing the data obtained and generating relevant conclusions and observations.

Research Paper (200 points)
Write a research paper on one of the following topics (or one that is pre-approved by the instructor). Your research paper should be five or more pages in length (word processed, 12-point font, double spaced, 1-inch margins on top bottom and sides). Include a reference page citing a minimum of six references from the professional literature (with emphasis on articles appearing in refereed journals). A rubric will be provided to specify guidelines and grading expectations.

Video Reviews (200 points possible)
Watch eight DVDs that relate to the topic/content of this course. Provide a written review of each DVD using the approved format.

Read One of the Following Books (200 points possible)
(Students are provided with a list of fiction/nonfiction texts that amplify course content) Write a three-page essay containing the following components: 1) basic thesis of the book, 2) a section of the book that had the greatest impact on you as a person, 3) applications and connections to your understanding of course content, and 4) implications of this book for you as a person.

Shadow a Professional in the Field (200 points possible)
Shadow a professional in the area or field of human services that you are considering as a focus for your vocation/calling. Journal/blog your experiences and those insights.

Develop a Resource Notebook (150 points possible)
Develop a resource notebook of materials that will be useful to you. The resource notebook should be a minimum of 100 pages of content selected from a variety of sources. Organize these resources with topical dividers.

Share A Motivational Comment with the Class (150 points)
As a means of integrating your newly acquired knowledge and information, prepare an inspirational thought for presentation to the class. The presentation should be 5-7 minutes in length and may take the form of a story, illustration, interpretive reading, song, dramatic presentation, etc. Make a connection between course content, the topic of your presentation, and a life application. A rubric will be provided. This assignment can be completed individually or in a group of two or three.

Create a PowerPoint Presentation (150 points)
Take some aspect of course content and develop a PowerPoint presentation that illustrates an important principle or concept. The presentation can only include a maximum of 10 pictures and 25 words. Be creative.

Provide Volunteer Experiences (150 points)
Provide 15 hours of volunteer services related to course content. Maintain a journal describing the nature of your volunteer services and the things that you are experiencing and learning.

Design Your Own Project (To be determined)
Submit a written description that includes the following components: (a) summary of project activities, (b) estimated time expenditure, and (c) method/product for sharing result

Figure 7.1. Sample evaluation menu. Reprinted from *A Brief Guide for Teaching Millennial Learners* by J. B. Garner, 2007, p. 22. Copyright 2007 by Triangle Publishing. Used with permission.

Rubrics provide learners with a clear picture of what is expected from them and help in planning and executing the final result of their efforts. Andrade (2005) describes the results of effective rubric use in her college classes:

> Instructional rubrics help my students understand the goal of an assignment and focus their efforts. I often cocreate a rubric with students by discussing strong and weak examples of student work with them, asking them to brainstorm criteria for their own work, and using the resulting list to write a draft rubric for their comment As a result, I never hear a student complain that she "didn't know what I wanted." (p. 29)

Like Andrade, Anderson (1998) advocates involving students in the assessment process and has proposed the four-by-four method as a way of engaging students in the development of rubrics:

1. In small groups, students identify four characteristics of good quality in the task they are completing. For example, the task might be a piece of writing, a classroom presentation, a double-entry journal, or a group project. In a writing task, the four characteristics could include introduction/closing, sources of information, organization, and grammar/spelling.
2. Each group writes four characteristics on a chalkboard or whiteboard.
3. One reporter from each group discusses one characteristic from the four characteristics, perhaps the one the group discussed the most or had the greatest passion about. As facilitators, instructors can help identify similarities and differences between the groups' criteria.
4. After each group has shared its criteria, the instructor asks the entire class to reach consensus about four criteria to be used when grading the task.
5. In small groups, students write four descriptors with a corresponding score for each of the four criteria. The scores range from 1 to 4, with 4 being the highest score.
6. After each group has shared its criteria, the class reaches group consensus. (p. 12)

Rubrics are helpful for any assignment involving some level of judgment in assessing the quality of student work along any number of dimensions. As a way of making this task easier and more consistent, there are a number of online resources that develop assessment rubrics for multiple types of assignments, including papers, presentations, digital assignments, collaborative group work, interviews, lab reports, and debates (see appendix).

Portfolio Assessments

Portfolios are longitudinal collections of student work, generally assembled in accordance with a specified set of criteria and content. Portfolios (or ePortfolios if done in a digital format) provide a summative description of the student's journey over the course of a semester and provide a snapshot for assessing growth and progress. According to Lombardi (2008), in addition to simply serving as a collection of materials and artifacts, the portfolio can also provide an opportunity for students to reflect on summative questions about their experiences and areas of growth (e.g., The most important lessons I learned..., Insights that I have gained..., The artifact I value the most is...).

In the first-year seminar, the portfolio provides a great way of helping students synthesize their experiences, successes, and challenges from their first semester in higher education. The materials included in this portfolio may include some of the assignments that were previously submitted and graded and a format for students to reflect on and evaluate their growth, insights, and plans for the future.

Connecting Points

Assessment is a critically important part of teaching and learning. This process allows faculty to observe the level at which students have grasped the knowledge, skills, and dispositions that have been identified as important in the first-year seminar. This information sheds light on the degree to which students have learned, but also provides faculty with a means for determining the effectiveness of chosen instructional pedagogies.

Just as students have different styles of learning, they also have preferred, and more effective ways, of demonstrating what they have learned. A high-quality assessment schema provides students with multiple ways of demonstrating their competence. Additionally, quality assessment practices promote higher level thinking and the application of acquired content to a variety of problems and circumstances. Assessment opportunities should be planned intentionally and built into the schedule and flow of the semester.

Appendix

Course Enhancement Resources

The following technological resources will assist you in the creation of an engaging environment for learning in the first-year seminar.

Electronic Professional Development

The Toolbox is an electronic professional development newsletter published by the National Resource Center for The First-Year Experience and Students in Transition. Published six times a year, this newsletter features classroom resources and teaching techniques and is available at www.sc.edu/fye/toolbox.

What Are They Thinking?

It is easy to lose touch with the thoughts and perspectives of new groups of students as they emerge from high school each year. On an annual basis, Beloit College publishes *The Mindset List*, an online resource capturing many of the key events and cultural perspectives common to students as they graduate from high school and prepare to enter college (starting with the members of the class of 2002, born in 1980). As an example, for the graduating class of 2015, born in 1993, *Amazon* has always been more than a river and an *Arnold Palmer* has always been a drink. *The Mindset List* can provide a better sense of the cultural contexts and experiences in the lives of your students (http://www.beloit.edu/mindset/).

Classroom Polling

A strategy to engage students in the expression of their opinions is electronic polling. By using their cell phones, students can register their thoughts and opinions to faculty-created polls. The emerging live results can be projected onto a screen. This approach often generates lively discussions on issues of concern. The website (www.polleverywhere.com) provides free access to groups under 30 students.

Did You Really Say That?

The process of copying and pasting the written word, whether original text or words or thoughts belonging to someone else, has become an increasingly common practice in college classes. To help students learn when to properly cite a source and avoid plagiarism, introduce them to plagiarism detection software (http://www.scanmyessay.com/plagiarism-free-software.php) and encourage them to use this resource in advance of submitting an assignment. Faculty can also use this tool to check student submissions that appear to be suspicious.

Glog About It

A glog (i.e., graphic blog) can offer your students a creative venue for expressing their thoughts and ideas in an online interactive poster format. Students can register for free on the website (http://edu.glogster.com/what-is-glogster-edu/) and create an electronic poster on a topic of interest by inserting images, photos, audio, video, and special effects. The results can be reviewed online and linked to social media sites.

Rubric Development

Creating rubrics is often a tedious and challenging task. Tools for designing rubrics for a variety of assignments (e.g., writing, mathematics, art, science, music, group projects) are available online at http://rubistar.4teachers.org/. The rubrics can be downloaded in an Excel format for editing and personalization.

Video Extraction

Consider the remarkable number of videos available on YouTube as teaching resources. These videos can be accessed in the classroom directly through an Internet connection using a hyperlink or by downloading a software tool that bypasses the variability of Internet connection strength and translates videos into a format that can be inserted directly into a PowerPoint slide (i.e., wmv or mp4). There are several programs available (for free or a minimal cost), including Tubesock (www.stinkbot.com) and the YouTube Video Converter (http://download.cnet.com/YouTube-Video-Converter/3000-2194_4-10720170.html). This technique provides a seamless way to make topically relevant video clips part of your classroom learning.

Wikis as a Collaborative Learning Environment

A wiki is an open-source website where participants can collaboratively create and edit the content of a document. For faculty, this creates the opportunity for groups of students to work together asynchronously on an assigned task. The mechanism also provides a means to track the level at which each participant contributed to the final product (i.e., number and extent of entries and edits).

Wikis are becoming a common feature on many learning management systems (e.g., Blackboard, Moodle). Faculty can also create wiki-based assignments using freestanding wikis where access is limited to identified members of the group. For more information, visit http://www.wikispaces.com/.

Online Discussion Forums

Social media is one of the signature technological developments of the 21st century and can be used as an effective tool to engage students in sharing their thoughts and feelings on course topics and issues. This can be accomplished in a variety of ways:

» *Facebook Discussion Group*—It is possible to create a discussion group on Facebook and restrict access to your students; simply log on to Facebook and click the *Create a Group* link. The easy access and students' familiarity with Facebook can encourage a high level of constructive engagement in this conversational format.

» *Blogs*—Another popular location for online conversation is the *blog* (i.e., a blend of the words *web* and *log*). As with other web tools, access to the blog can be restricted to the members of a designated class group. Faculty can provide prompts and then require students to make a specified number of entries and responses within a given timeframe. Directions for creating a Google blog can be found at http://www.ehow.com/how_4866981_create-blog-google.html.

Keep Looking and Learning

This appendix describes only a few of the many resources available on the Internet that can provide enhanced learning opportunities for students. Online possibilities and technologies rapidly change in the cyber world, which requires faculty to frequently browse, search, and experiment to remain abreast of new developments and continue to learn new skills that will help students effectively and efficiently reach course and program learning outcomes. Learning can and should be a lifelong endeavor for both the instructor and the student.

References

Abrami, P. C. (1995). *Classroom connections: Understanding and using cooperative learning.* Toronto, Canada: Harcourt Brace.

Agarwal, P. K., Karpicke, J. D., Kang, S. K., Roediger, H. L., & McDermott, K. B. (2008). Examining the testing effect with open- and closed-book tests. *Applied Cognitive Psychology, 22*(7), 861-876.

American Association of Colleges and Universities (AAC&U). (1995). *The drama of diversity and democracy: Higher education and American commitments.* Washington D. C.: Author.

Anderson, C. F. (2006). Why teaching first-year seminars is rewarding for everyone. *Peer Review, 8*(3), 20-22.

Anderson, R. S. (1998). Why talk about different ways to grade? The shift from traditional to alternative assessment. In R. S. Anderson & B. W. Speck (Eds.), *Classroom assessment and the new learning paradigm* (New Directions in Teaching and Learning, No. 74, pp. 5-16). San Francisco, CA: Jossey-Bass.

Anderson, L. W., & Krathwohl, D. R. (Eds.). (2001). *A taxonomy for learning, teaching and assessing: A revision of Bloom's Taxonomy of educational objectives: Complete edition.* New York, NY: Longman.

Andrade, G. H. (2005). Teaching with rubrics: The good, the bad, and the ugly. *College Teaching, 53*(1), 27-30.

Angelo, T. A., & Cross, K. P. (1993). *Classroom assessment techniques.* San Francisco, CA: Jossey-Bass.

Archibold, R. C. (1998, April 25). Yes, teacher: Giuliani scolds CUNY on attendance. *New York Times*, p. B4.

Aronson, E. (n.d.). *Overview of the technique.* Retrieved from the Jigsaw Classroom website http://www.jigsaw.org/overview.htm

Aronson, E., Stephan, C., Sikes, J., Blaney, N., & Snapp, M. (1978). *The jigsaw classroom.* Beverly Hills, CA: Sage Publications.

Backes, C., & Brown, P. (2009). Going beyond the test! Using alternative assessments in career education. *Techniques: Connecting Education & Careers, 84*(3), 34-37.

Bain, K. (2004). *What the best college teachers do.* Cambridge, MA: Harvard University Press.

Bangert, A. (2004). The seven principles of good practice: A framework for evaluating online teaching. *Internet & Higher Education, 7*(3), 217-232.

Barack, L. (2006). Digital textbooks for digital natives. *School Library Journal, 52*(2), 24.

Barr, R. B. (1998). Obstacles to implementing the learning paradigm. *About Campus, 3*(4), 18-25.

Barr, R. B. (2003). *The learning paradigm college.* Bolton, MA: Anker Publishing.

Barr, R. B., & Tagg, J. (1995). From teaching to learning—A new paradigm for undergraduate education. *Change, 27*(6), 12-25.

Basham, G. & Nardone, H. (1997). Using the film JFK to teach critical thinking. *College Teaching, 45*(1),10-13.

Bauerlein, M. (2008). *The dumbest generation: How the digital age stupefies young Americans and jeopardizes our future.* New York, NY: Tarcher/Penguin.

Baxter Magolda, M. B. (2000). *Creating contexts for learning and self-authorship: Constructive-developmental pedagogy.* Nashville, TN: Vanderbilt University Press.

Becker, A., & Calhoon, S. (1999). What introductory psychology students attend to on a course syllabus. *Teaching of Psychology, 26*(1), 6-11.

Bjorklund, W., & Rehling, D. (2010). Student perceptions of classroom incivility. *College Teaching, 58*(1), 15-18.

Bligh, D. A. (2000). *What's the use of lectures?* San Francisco, CA: Jossey-Bass.

Bloom, B. S. (Ed.). (1956). *Taxonomy of educational objectives, handbook I: The cognitive domain.* New York, NY: David McKay Co Inc.

Bloom, D. (2009). Collaborative test taking: Benefits for learning and retention. *College Teaching, 57*(4), 216-220.

Bluestone, C. (2000). Feature films as a teaching tool. *College Teaching, 48*(4), 141-146.

Bonwell, C. C., & Eisen, J. A. (1991). *Active learning: Creating excitement in the classroom* (ASHE-ERIC Higher Education Report No. 1). Washington, DC: The George Washington University, School of Education and Human Development.

Borst, J., Taatgen, N., & van Rijn, H. (2010). The problem state: A cognitive bottleneck in multitasking. *Journal of Experimental Psychology / Learning, Memory & Cognition, 36*(2), 363-382.

Bostock, S. J. (1998). Constructivism in mass higher education. *British Journal of Educational Technology, 29*, 225-240.

Brown, J. (2010). Can you hear me now? *T+D, 64*(2), 28-30.

Buechner, F. (1983). *Now and then: A memoir of vocation.* New York, NY: Harper.

Bugeja, M. (2007, January 26). Distractions in the wireless classroom. *Chronicle of Higher Education*, pp. C1, C4.

Burgan, M. (2006). In defense of lecturing. *Change, 38*(6), 30-34.

Burgess, M., & Caverly, D. (2009). Techtalk: Second Life and developmental education. *Journal of Developmental Education, 32*(3), 42-43.

Caboni, T., Mundy, M., & Duesterhaus, M. (2002). The implications of the norms of undergraduate college students for faculty enactment of principles of good practice in undergraduate education. *Peabody Journal of Education, 77*(3), 125-137.

Cahn, S. M. (1994). Rethinking examinations and grades. In P. J. Markie (Ed.), *A professor's duties: Ethical issues in college teaching,* (pp. 171-192). Lanham, MD: Rowman and Littlefield.

Cameron, B. J. (1991). Using tests to teach. *College Teaching, 39*(4), 154-156.

Caverly, D., Ward, A., & Caverly, M. (2009). Techtalk: Mobile learning and access. *Journal of Developmental Education, 33*(1), 38-39.

Chanen, J. (2007). Profs kibosh students' laptops. *ABA Journal, 93*(11), 16.

Chen, X. (2002). *Teaching undergraduates in U.S. postsecondary institutions: Fall 1998.* Washington, DC : National Center for Education Statistics.

Chesler, M., Lewis, A., & Crowfoot, J. (2005). *Challenging racism in higher education: Promoting justice.* Lanham, MD: Rowman & Littlefield Publishers.

Chickering, A. W., & Ehrmann, S. C. (1996). Implementing the seven principles: Technology as lever. *AAHE Bulletin, 49*(2), 3-6.

Chickering, A. W., & Gamson, Z. F. (1987). Seven principles for good practice in undergraduate education. *AAHE Bulletin, 39*(7), 3–7.

Chickering, A. W., & Gamson, Z. F. (1999). Development and adaptations of the seven principles for good practice in undergraduate education. In M. D. Svinicki (Ed.), *Teaching on the edge of the millennium: Building on what we have learned* (New Directions for Teaching & Learning, No. 80, pp. 75-81). San Francisco, CA: Jossey-Bass.

Chronicle Research Services. (2009). *The college of 2020: Students.* Washington, DC: Author.

Chun, E., & Evans, A. (2009). *Bridging the diversity divide.* San Francisco, CA: Jossey-Bass.

Chun, M. (2010). Taking teaching to (performance) task: Linking pedagogical and assessment practices. *About Campus, 42*(2), 22-29.

Clump, M., Bauer, H., & Bradley, C. (2004). The extent to which psychology students read textbooks: A multiple class analysis of reading across the psychology curriculum. *Journal of Instructional Psychology, 31*(3), 227-232.

Clump, M. A., Bauer, H., & Whiteleather, A. (2003). To attend or not to attend: Is that a good question? *Journal of Instructional Psychology, 30*(3), 220-224.

Colosimo, M. (2004). How shall we learn? How shall we live? *Phi Kappa Phi Forum, 84*(4), 32-33.

Connor-Greene, P. A. (2000). Assessing and promoting student learning: Blurring the line between teaching and testing. *Teaching of Psychology, 27*, 84-88.

Coomes, M. D., & DeBard, R. (2004). A generational approach to understanding students. In M.D. Coomes & R. DeBard (Eds.), *Serving the millennial generation* (New Directions for Student Services, No. 106, pp. 5-16). San Francisco, CA: Jossey-Bass.

Cooper, K. J. (2009). IT: Intellectually taxing? *Diverse: Issues in Higher Education, 26*(3), 11-12.

Cordell, R. (2011, May 13). New technologies to get your students engaged. *Chronicle of Higher Education*, pp. B8, B10.

Cox, B. E., & Orehovec, E. (2007). Faculty-student interaction outside the classroom: A typology from a residential college. *The Review of Higher Education, 30*(4), 343-362.

Dale, E. (1946). *Audio-visual methods in teaching.* New York, NY: The Dryden Press.

Davies, M. A., & Wavering, M. (1999). Alternative assessment: New directions in teaching and learning. *Contemporary Education, 71*, 39-46.

Deahl, R. (2010, November 1). How e-book sales compare to print... so far. *Publishers Weekly*, 4.

Dewey, J. (1937). *Experience and education.* New York, NY: Scribner.

Diamond, R. M. (1998). *Designing and assessing courses and curricula.* San Francisco, CA: Jossey-Bass.

Diaz-Lefebvre, R. (2004). Multiple intelligences, learning for understanding, and creative assessment: Some pieces to the puzzle of learning. *Teachers College Record, 106*, 49-57.

Dittmer, J. (2010). Immersive virtual worlds in university-level human geography courses. *International Research in Geographical & Environmental Education, 19*(2), 139-154.

Dolmans, D., De Grave, W., Wolfhagen, I., & van der Vleuten, C. (2005). Problem-based learning: future challenges for educational practice and research. *Medical Education, 39*(7), 732-741.

Duch, B. J. (2001). Writing problems for deeper understanding. In B. J. Duch, S. E. Groh, & D. E. Allen (Eds.), *The power of problem-based learning* (pp. 47-58). Sterling, VA: Stylus.

Duch, B. J., Groh, S. E., & Allen, D. E. (2001). Why problem-based learning? A case study of institutional change in undergraduate education. In B. J. Duch, S. E. Groh, & D. E. Allen (Eds.), *The power of problem-based learning* (pp. 3-12). Sterling, VA: Stylus.

Duderstadt, J. J. (1999). Can colleges and universities survive in the information age? In R. N. Katz & Associates (Eds.), *Dancing with the devil: Information technology and the new competition in higher education* (pp. 1-26). San Francisco, CA: Jossey-Bass.

Dunbar, N., Brooks, C., & Kubicka-Miller, T. (2006). Oral communication skills in higher education: Using a performance-based evaluation rubric to assess communication skills. *Innovative Higher Education, 31*(2), 115-128.

Edgerton, R. (2001, March 6). *White paper on higher education*. Washington, DC: Pew Forum on Undergraduate Education. Retrieved from www.faculty.umb.edu/.../Edgerton%20Higher%20Education%20White%20Paper.rtf

Eimers, M., Braxton, J., & Bayer, A. (2001). Normative support for improving undergraduate education in teaching-oriented colleges. *Research in Higher Education, 42*(5), 569-592.

Engstrom, C. M., & Tinto, V. (1997). Working together for service learning. *About Campus, 2*(3), 10-15.

Erickson, B. L., Peters, C. B., & Strommer, D. W. (2006). *Teaching first-year college students*. San Francisco, CA: Jossey-Bass.

Evenbeck, S. (2006, November). *Centering on students*. Paper presented at the 13th Annual Conference on Student Transition, St. Louis, MO.

Eyler, J. (2009). The power of experiential education. *Liberal Education, 95*(4), 24-31.

Fear, F. A., Doberneck, C. F., Robinson, C. F., Fear, K. L., Barr, R. B., Van Den Berg, H., Smith, J., & Petrulis, R. (2003). Meaning making and "The Learning Paradigm": A provocative idea in practice. *Innovative Higher Education, 27*(3), 151-168.

Fleming, C. T., & Garner, J. B. (2009). *A brief guide to teaching adult learners*. Marion, IN: Triangle Publishing.

Freire, P. (1974). *Pedagogy of the oppressed*. New York, NY: Seabury.

Fried, C. B. (2008). In-class laptop use and its effects on student learning. *Computers & Education, 50*(3), 906-914.

Gahagan, J., Dingfelder, J., & Pei, K. (2010). *A faculty and staff guide to creating learning outcomes*. Columbia, SC: University of South Carolina, National Resource Center for The First-Year Experience.

Gaither, G. H. (2005). Editor's notes. In G. H. Gaither (Ed.), *Minority retention: What works?* (New Directions for Institutional Research, No. 125, pp. 1-5). San Francisco, CA: Jossey-Bass.

Galles, M., & Olson, P. J. (2008). A new method of linking courses: A theologian and a sociologist share their experience. *Innovative Higher Education, 33*, 39-48.

Gardner, D. S., Tuchman, E., & Hawkins, R. (2010). Teaching note: A cross-curricular, problem-based project to promote understanding of poverty in urban communities. *Journal of Social Work Education, 46*(1), 147-156.

Garmston, R. J., & Wellman, B. M. (1999). *The adaptive school: A sourcebook for developing collaborative groups*. Norwood, MA: Christopher-Gordon Publishers.

Garmston, R. J., & Wellman, B. M. (2002). *The adaptive school: Developing collaborative groups*. Norwood, MA: Christopher-Gordon Publishers.

Garner, J. B. (2007). *A brief guide to teaching millennial learners*. Marion, IN: Triangle Publishing.

Garner, J. B. (2010, September). Problem-based learning: A strategy for enhancing the relevance connection. *The Toolbox, 9*(1).

Gasser, U., & Palfrey, J. (2009). Mastering multitasking. *Educational Leadership, 66*(6), 14-19.

Gier, V., & Kreiner, D. (2009). Incorporating active learning with PowerPoint-based lectures using content-based questions. *Teaching of Psychology, 36*(2), 134-139.

Giroux, H. (1992). *Border crossings*. London, UK: Routledge.

Goodman, B. (2009). Love it or loathe it. *Nursing Standard, 23*(30), 61.

Goodman, K., & Pascarella, E. T. (2006). First-year seminars increase persistence and retention: A summary of the evidence from how college affects students. *Peer Review, 8*(3), 26-28.

Graham, J. (2006). Blended learning systems: Definition, current trends, and future directions. In C. J. Bonk & C. R. Graham (Eds.), *The handbook of blended learning: Global perspectives, local designs* (pp. 3-21). San Francisco, CA: Pfeiffer.

Grossman, R. (2009). Structure for student reflection. *College teaching, 57*(1), 15-22.

Gump, S. (2005). The cost of cutting class: Attendance as a predictor of student success. *College Teaching, 53*(1), 21-26.

Gurin, P., Dey, E., Gurin, G., & Hurtado, S. (2003). How does racial/ethnic diversity promote education? *Western Journal of Black Studies, 27*(1), 20-29.

Habanek, D. (2005). An examination of the integrity of the syllabus. *College Teaching, 53*(2), 62-64.

Haladyna, T. M., Downing, S. M., & Rodriguez, M. C. (2002). A review of multiple-choice item-writing guidelines for classroom assessment. *Applied Measurement in Education, 15*, 309-334.

Heath, M. R. (2011). *Strong growth ahead for Twitter based on the experience of mobile SMS*. Retrieved from http://www.ezinearticles.com

Hew, K. (2009). Use of audio podcast in K-12 and higher education: A review of research topics and methodologies. *Educational Technology Research & Development, 57*(3), 333-357.

Higher Education Opportunity Act of 1008, Public Law 110-315 (2008).

Howe, N., & Strauss, W. (1992). *Generations: The history of America's future, 1584 to 2069*. New York, NY: Harper.

Howe, N., & Strauss, W. (2000). *Millennials rising: The next great generation*. New York, NY: Random House.

Howe, N., & Strauss, W. (2003). *Millennials go to college*. Washington, DC: American Association of Collegiate Registrars.

Howe, N., & Strauss, W. (2006). *Millennials and pop culture*. Great Falls, VA: Life-Course Associates.

Hunter, M. S., & Linder, C. W. (2005). First-year seminars. In M. L. Upcraft, J. N. Gardner, B. O. Barefoot, & Associates (Eds.), *Challenging and supporting the first-year student: A handbook for improving the first year of college* (pp. 275- 291). San Francisco, CA: Jossey- Bass.

Hussey, T., & Smith, P. (2010). Transitions in higher education. *Innovations in Education & Teaching International, 47*(2), 155-164.

Johnson, D. W., & Johnson, R. T. (1993). *Cooperation in the classroom*. Alexandria, VA: Association for Supervision and Curriculum Development.

Johnson, D. W., & Johnson, R. T. (1998a). Cooperative learning returns to college: What evidence is there that it works? *Change, 30*(4), 26-35.

Johnson, D. W., & Johnson, R. T. (1998b). *Active learning: Cooperation in the college classroom* (2nd ed.). Edna, MN: Interaction Books.

Jones, W. T. (2005). The realities of diversity and the campus climate for first-year students. In M. L. Upcraft, J. N. Gardner, B. O. Barefoot, & Associates (Eds.), *Challenging and supporting the first-year student: A handbook for improving the first year of college* (pp. 141-155). San Francisco, CA: Jossey-Bass.

Jung, I., & Suzuki, K. (2006). Blended learning in Japan and its application in liberal arts education. In C. J. Bonk & C. R. Graham (Eds.), *The handbook of blended learning: Global perspectives, local designs* (pp. 267-280). San Francisco, CA: Pfeiffer.

Kagan, S. (1994). *Cooperative learning*. San Clemente, CA: Kagan Publishing Company.

Kazanjian, V. H. (2000). Beyond tolerance: From mono-religious to multi-religious life at Wellesley College. In V. Kazjanian & P. Laurence (Eds.), *Education as transformation: Religious pluralism, spirituality, and a new vision for higher education in America* (pp. 213-230). New York, NY: Peter Land Publishers.

Kegan, R. (1994). *In over our heads: The mental demands of modern life*. Cambridge, MA: Harvard University Press.

Keeling, R. (Ed.). (2004). *Learning reconsidered: A campus-wide focus on the student experience*. Washington, DC: National Association of Student Personnel Administrators and American College Personnel Association.

Kember, D., & Gow, L. (1994). Orientations to teaching and their effect on the quality of student learning. *The Journal of Higher Education, 65*(1), 58-74.

Kennedy, M. (2009, March 1). Crisis communication. *American School & University*, 16.

Keup, J. R. (2008). New challenges in working with traditional-aged college students. In B. O. Barefoot (Ed.), *The first year and beyond: Rethinking the challenge of collegiate transition* (pp. 27-37). San Francisco, CA: Jossey-Bass.

Kingsbury, A., & Galloway, L. (2006, October 16). Textbooks enter the digital era. *U.S. News & World Report*, 63-65.

Kinsella, S. (2009). Many to one: Using the mobile phone to interact with large classes. *British Journal of Educational Technology, 40*(5), 956-958.

Klemm, W. R. (2007). Computer slide shows: A trap for bad teaching. *College Teaching, 55*(3), 121-124.

Knowles, M. S. (1984). *The adult learner: A neglected species* (3rd ed.). Houston, TX: Gulf Publishing Company.

Kolb, D. A. (1984). *Experiential learning: Experience as the source of learning and development*. Englewood Cliffs, NJ: Prentice-Hall.

Korchmaros, J., & Gump, N. (2009). Evaluation of using course-management software. *College Teaching, 57*(3), 161-166.

Kuh, G. D. (2008). *High-impact educational practices: What they are, who has access to them, and why they matter*. Washington, DC: Association of American Colleges and Universities.

Kuh, G. D. (2009a). The National Survey of Student Engagement: Conceptual and empirical foundations. *New Directions for Institutional Research, 141*, 5-20.

Kuh, G. D. (2009b). What student affairs professionals need to know about student engagement. *Journal of College Student Development, 50*, 683-706.

Kuh, G. D., Douglas, K. B., Lund, J. P., & Ramin-Gyurnek, J. (1994). *Student learning outside the classroom: Transcending artificial boundaries* (ASHE-ERIC Report No. 8). Washington, DC: The George Washington University, Graduate School of Education.

Kuh, G. D. , Kinzie, J., Schuh, J. H. , Whitt, E. J., & Associates. (2005). *Student success in college: Creating conditions that matter*. San Francisco, CA: Jossey-Bass.

Kuh, G. D., Schuh, J. H., Whitt, E. J., & Associates. (1991). *Involving colleges: Successful approaches to fostering student learning and development outside the classroom*. San Francisco, CA: Jossey-Bass.

Lalley, J., & Miller, R. (2007). The learning pyramid: Does it point teachers in the right direction? *Education, 128*(1), 64-79.

Lang, J. (2006, September 1). The promising syllabus. *Chronicle of Higher Education*, p. B114.

Lavin, A. M., Korte, L., & Davies, T. L. (2010). The impact of classroom technology on student behavior. *Journal of Technology Research, 2*, 1-13.

Levine, A., & Cureton, J. S. (1998). *When hope and fear collide: A portrait of today's college student*. San Francisco, CA: Jossey-Bass.

Lewis, C. C., & Abdul-Hamid, H. (2006). Implementing effective online teaching practices: Voices of exemplary faculty. *Innovative Higher Education, 31*(2), 83-98.

Liles, R. (2007). The use of feature films as teaching tools in social work education. *Journal of Teaching in Social Work, 27*(3/4), 45-60.

Lombardi, J. (2008). To portfolio or not to portfolio: Helpful or hyped? *College Teaching, 56*(1), 7-10.

Lum, L. (2006, March 9). The power of podcasting. *Diverse Issues in Higher Education*, 32-35.

MacBeath, J. (2006). Finding voice, finding self. *Educational Review, 58*(2), 195-207.

Magna Publications. (2005, June 1). *Online classroom: Interactive syllabus improves course accessibility*. Retrieved from http://www.magnapubs.com/newsletter/issue/514/

Marklin Reynolds, J., & Hancock, D. (2010). Problem-based learning in a higher education environmental biotechnology course. *Innovations in Education & Teaching International, 47*(2), 175-186.

Masikunis, G., Panayiotidis, A., & Burke, L. (2009). Changing the nature of lectures using a personal response system. *Innovations in Education & Teaching International, 46*(2), 199-212.

Mazer, J. P., Murphy, R. E., & Simonds, C. J. (2009). The effects of teacher self-disclosure via Facebook on teacher credibility. *Learning, Media, and Technology, 34*(2), 175-183.

McDaniel, T. R. (1994). College classrooms of the future. *College Teaching, 94*, 27-32.

McGill, T. J., & Hobbs, V. J. (2008). How students and instructors using a virtual learning environment perceive the fit between technology and task. *Journal of Computer Assisted Learning, 28*, 191-202.

McKinney, J., McKinney, K., Franiuk, R., & Schweitzer, J. (2006). The college classroom as a community. *College Teaching, 54*(3), 281-284.

McLeod, W. B., & Young, J. M. (2005). Establishing an institutional culture of student success. In G. H. Gaither (Ed.), *Minority retention: What works?* (pp. 73-86). San Francisco, CA: Jossey-Bass.

Merriam, S., & Caffarella, R. (1999). *Learning in adulthood: A comprehensive guide* (2nd ed.). San Francisco, CA: Jossey-Bass.

Mestre, J. P. (2005). Facts and myths about pedagogies of engagement in science learning. *Peer Review, 7*(2), 24-27.

Milton, O. (1986). *Will that be on the final?* Springfield, IL: Charles C. Thomas.

Montgomery, K. (2002). Authentic tasks and rubrics: Going beyond traditional assessments in college teaching. *College Teaching, 50*(1), 34-39.

Moore, R. (2003). Attendance and performance: How important is it for students to attend class? *Journal of College Science Teaching, 32*(6), 367-371.

Moroni, A. S., & Tarr, T. A. (2005). Theoretical eclecticism in the college classroom. *Innovative Higher Education, 30*(1), 7-21.

Moss, K., & Crowley, M. (2011). Effective learning in science: The use of personal response systems with a wide range of audiences. *Computers & Education, 56*(1), 36-43.

Murray, J. P. (1990). Better testing for better learning. *College Teaching, 38*, 148-153.

National Center for Educational Statistics (NCES). (2004). *National household education surveys of 2001: Participation in adult education and lifelong learning: 2000-01.* Washington, DC: U.S. Department of Education.

National Center for Public Policy and Higher Education. (2008). *Partnerships for public purposes: Engaging higher education in societal challenges of the 21st century.* Washington, DC: Author.

Newlin, M. H., & Wang, A. Y. (2002). Integrating technology and pedagogy: Web instruction and seven principles of undergraduate education. *Teaching of Psychology, 29*(4), 325-330.

Nilson, L. B. (2007). *The graphic syllabus and the outcomes map: Communicating your course.* San Francisco, CA: Jossey-Bass.

Nilson, L. B., & Biktimorov, E. B. (2003). Mapping your course: Developing a graphic syllabus for introductory finance. *Journal of Education for Business, 78*(6), 308-312.

Palmer, P. J. (1997). *The courage to teach: Exploring the inner landscape of a teacher's life.* Hoboken, NJ: John Wiley & Sons.

Palmer, P. J. (1999). *Let your life speak: Listening for the voice of vocation.* San Francisco, CA: Jossey-Bass.

Panday, P. P. (2007). Simplifying podcasting. *International Journal of Teaching and Learning in Higher Education, 20*(2), 251-261.

Parkyn, D. L. (1999). Learning in the company of others. *College Teaching, 47,* 88-90.

Pascarella, E. T., & Terenzini, P. T. (2005). *How college affects students* (Vol. 2). San Francisco, CA: Jossey-Bass.

Pattengale, J., & Garner, J. B. (2007, February). *The wiki world of first-year students: Finding creative ways to use millennial preferences for their own success.* Presented at the Annual Conference on The First-Year Experience, Addison, TX.

Pennell, M., & Miles, L. (2009). It actually made me think: Problem-based learning in the business communications classroom. *Business Communication Quarterly, 72*(4), 377-394.

Petress, K. (1996). The dilemma of university undergraduate student attendance policies: To require class attendance or not. *College Student Journal, 30*(3), 387.

Pingdom. (2010, January 22). *Internet 2009 in numbers.* Retrieved from http://royal.pingdom.com/2010/01/22/internet-2009-in-numbers/

Porter, S. R., & Swing, R. L. (2006). Understanding how first-year seminars affect persistence. *Research in Higher Education, 47*(1), 90-109.

Postholm, M. B. (2008). Group work as a learning situation: a qualitative study in a university classroom *Teachers and Teaching: Theory and Practice, 14*(2), 143–155.

Pray S. M., & Tracy, D. M. (1999). Collaborative essay testing. *College Teaching, 47*(1), 33-36.

Prensky, M. (2001). Digital natives, digital immigrants. *On the Horizon, 9*(5), 1-6.

Pursell, D. (2009). Adapting to student learning styles: Engaging students with cell phone technology in organic chemistry instruction. *Journal of Chemical Education, 86*(10), 1219-1222.

Raab, L., & Adam, A. J. (2005). The university college model: A learning-centered approach to retention and remediation. In G. H. Gaither (Ed.), *Minority retention: What works?* (pp. 87-106). San Francisco, CA: Jossey- Bass.

Read, B. (2005, October 28). Lectures on the go: As more colleges use "coursecasting", professors are split on its place in teaching. *The Chronicle of Higher Education*, p. A39.

Rheem, J. (1998). Problem-based learning: An introduction. *National Teaching and Learning Forum, 8*(1), 1-4.

Rhoads, R. A. (1997). Classrooms without walls, students without limits. *About Campus, 2*(2), 28-30.

Rhoads, R. A., & Howard, J. P. F. (1998). Critical multiculturalism in service learning. In R. A. Rhoads & J. P. F. Howard (Eds.), *Academic service learning: A pedagogy of action and reflection.* (New Directions for Teaching and Learning, No. 73, pp. 39-46). San Francisco, CA: Jossey-Bass.

Richardson, W. (2006). *Blogs, wikis, podcasts and other powerful web tools for classrooms.* Thousand Oaks, CA: Corwin Press.

Ritter, M., & Lemke, K. (2000). Addressing the seven principles for good practice in undergraduate education with Internet-enhanced education. *Journal of Geography in Higher Education, 24*, 100-108.

Rosch, D., & Nocerino, T. (2007). Knowing the path and walking the path. *About Campus, 12*(5), 17-20.

Russo, A., & Warren, S. H. (1999). Collaborative test taking. *College Teaching, 47*, 18-20.

Salaway, G., Caruso, J. B., & Nelson, M. R. (2007). *The ECAR survey of undergraduate students and information technology, 2007.* Boulder, CO: Educause Center for Applied Research.

Sanders, L. R. (2001). Improving assessment in university classrooms. *College Teaching, 49*, 62-64.

Schroeder, C. (2003). What's going on in higher education? [Interview with Russell Edgerton] *About Campus, 8*(2), 8-15.

Scott, C. (2005, October 7). The net generation in the classroom. *Chronicle of Higher Education*, pp. A 34-37.

Selwyn, N. (2009). Faceworking: Exploring students' education-related use of Facebook. *Learning, Media, & Technology, 34*(2), 157-174.

Shang, P., & Barkis, M. (2009). The AISP model on increasingly diverse campuses. In R. Junco & D. M. Timm (Eds.), *Using emerging technologies to enhance student engagement* (New Directions for Student Services, No. 124, pp. 69-76). San Francisco, CA: Jossey-Bass.

Shank, P. (Ed.). (2007). *The online learning idea book*. San Francisco, CA: Pfeiffer.

Shepperd, J., Grace, J., & Koch, E. (2008). Evaluating the electronic textbook: Is it time to dispense with the paper text? *Teaching of Psychology, 35*(1), 2-5.

Shulman, L. S. (1993). Teaching as community property. *Change, 25*(6), 6-7.

Sikorski, J., Rich, K., Saville, B., Buskist, W., Drogan, O., & Davis, S. (2002). Student use of introductory texts: Comparative survey findings from two universities. *Teaching of Psychology, 29*(4), 312.

Silver, J. (Producer), & Wachowski, A., & Wachowski, L. (Directors). (1999). *The matrix* [Motion Picture]. United States: Village Roadshow Pictures.

Slattery, J. M. & Carlson, J. F. (2005). Preparing an effective syllabus. *College Teaching, 53*, 159-164.

Smith, L. E., MacGregor, J., Matthews, R. S., & Gabelnick, F. (2004). *Learning communities: Reforming undergraduate education*. San Francisco, CA: Jossey-Bass.

Smith, K. A., Sheppard, S. D., Johnson, D. W., & Johnson R. T. (2005). Pedagogies of engagement: Classroom-based practices. *Journal of Engineering Education, 94*, 87-101.

Spence, L. D. (2001). The case against teaching. *Change, 33*(6), 10-19.

Sporer, R. (2001). The no-fault quiz. *College Teaching, 49*(2), 61.

Stearns, S. A. (1996). Collaborative exams as learning tools. *College Teaching, 44*, 111-112.

Tagg, J. (2003). *The learning paradigm college*. Bolton, MA: Anker.

Thomas, D., & Brown, J. S. (2011). *A new culture of learning: Cultivating a culture of imagination in a world of constant change*. Seattle, WA: CreateSpace Publishing.

Thompson, B. (2002, June 21). If I quiz them, they will come. *Chronicle of Higher Education*, p. B5.

Uba, F. A. (2009). Surgical principles and problem-based learning in surgery: A revision guide. *African Journal of Paediatric Surgery, 6*(2), 143.

U.S. Department of Commerce. (2010). *Visions 2020.2: Student views on transforming education and training through advanced technologies*. Washington, DC: Author.

U.S. Department of Labor. (2007). *Adult learners in higher education: Barriers to success and strategies to improve results*. Washington, DC: Author.

VanBlerekom, M. L. (2001). Class attendance in undergraduate courses. *The Journal of Psychology, 126*(5), 487-494.

Wasley, P. (2008, March 14). The syllabus becomes a repository of legalese. *Chronicle of Higher Education*, pp. A1-A10.

Weaver, B., & Nilson, L. B. (2005, Spring). Laptops in class: What are they good for? What can you do with them? In L. B. Nilson & B. Weaver (Eds.), *Enhancing learning with laptops in the classroom* (New Directions for Teaching & Learning, No. 101, pp. 3-13). San Francisco, CA: Jossey-Bass.

Weigert, K. (1998). Academic service learning: Its meaning and relevance. In R. A. Rhoads & J. P. F. Howard (Eds.), *Academic service learning: A pedagogy of action and reflection* (New Directions for Teaching and Learning, No. 73, pp. 3-13). San Francisco, CA: Jossey-Bass.

Weimer, M. (2002). *Learner-centered teaching.* San Francisco, CA: Jossey-Bass.

Wergin, J. F. (1988). Basic issues and principles in classroom assessment. In J. H. McMillan (Ed.), *Assessing student's learning* (pp. 5-17). San Francisco, CA: Jossey-Bass.

Wilson, K. R., Wallin, J. S., & Reiser, C. (2003). Social stratification and the digital divide. *Social Science Computer Review, 21*(2), 133-143.

Young, J. R. (2003, April 18). Reclaiming Friday. *Chronicle of Higher Education*, p. A46.

Young, J. (2010). Teaching with Twitter. *Education Digest, 75*(7), 9-12.

Zlotkowski, E. (Ed.). (2001). *Service-learning and the first-year experience: Preparing students for personal success and civic responsibility* (Monograph No. 34). Columbia, SC: University of South Carolina, National Resource Center for The First-Year Experience and Students in Transition.

Index

NOTE: Page numbers with italicized *f* or *n* indicate figures or notes respectively.